DIARY

of a Wimpy Kid

小屁孩日记①

——鬼屋创意

[美] 杰夫·金尼 著

朱力安 译

格雷的"死党"
——罗利

格雷

·广州·

广东省出版集团

新世纪出版社

本书简体中文版由美国 Harry N. Abrams 公司通过中国 Creative Excellence Rights Agency 独家授权
版权合同登记号：19-2009-002 号

图书在版编目（CIP）数据

小屁孩日记①：鬼屋创意/（美）杰夫·金尼著；朱力安译.
—2 版. —广州：新世纪出版社，2009.3（2012.6 重印）
ISBN 978-7-5405-3913-9

Ⅰ.小… Ⅱ.①杰… ②朱… Ⅲ.日记体小说-美国-现代 Ⅳ.I712.45

中国版本图书馆 CIP 数据核字（2008）第 203532 号

出 版 人：孙泽军
选题策划：林　铨　王小斌
责任编辑：王小斌　傅　琨
责任技编：王建慧

小屁孩日记①——鬼屋创意
XIAOPIHAI RIJI①——GUIWU CHUANGYI
[美] 杰夫·金尼　著　朱力安　译

出版发行：新世纪出版社
　　　　　（广州市大沙头四马路 10 号　邮政编码：510102）
经　　销：全国新华书店
印　　刷：广州市至元印刷有限公司
开　　本：890mm×1240mm　1/32
印　　张：7　字　数：135 千字
版　　次：2009 年 3 月第 1 版　2012 年 6 月第 2 版
印　　次：2012 年 6 月第 20 次印刷
印　　数：232 001～237 000
定　　价：16.80 元

质量监督电话：020-83797655　购书咨询电话：020-83781545

格雷的老爸

格雷的老妈

格雷的哥哥
——罗德里克

格雷的同学
——弗雷格

格雷的弟弟
——曼尼

"小屁孩之父" 杰夫·金尼致中国粉丝

中国的"哈屁族":

你们好!

从小我就对中国很着迷,现在能给中国读者写信真是我的荣幸啊。我从来没想过自己会成为作家,更没想到我的作品会流传到你们的国家,一个离我家十万八千里的地方。

当我还是个小屁孩的时候,我和我的朋友曾试着挖地洞,希望一直挖下去就能到地球另一端的中国。不一会儿,我们就放弃了这个想法(要知道,挖洞是件多辛苦的事儿啊!);但现在通过我的这些作品,我终于到中国来了——只是通过另一种方式,跟我的想象有点不一样的方式。

谢谢你们让《小屁孩日记》在中国成为畅销书。我希望你们觉得这些故事是有趣的,也希望这些故事对你们是一种激励,让你们有朝一日也成为作家和漫画家。我是幸运的,因为我的梦想就是成为一个漫画家,而现在这个梦想实现了。不管你们的梦想是什么,我都希望你们梦想成真。

我希望有朝一日能亲身到中国看看。这是个将要实现的梦想!

希望你们喜欢《小屁孩日记》的第五册(编者注:即中译本第9、10册)。再次感谢你们对这套书的喜爱!

杰夫

A Letter to Chinese Readers

Hello to all my fans in China!

I've had a fascination with China ever since I was a boy, and it's a real privilege to be writing to you now. I never could have imagined that I would become an author, and that my work would reach a place as far from my home as your own country.

When I was a kid, my friends and I tried to dig a hole in the ground, because we hoped we could reach China on the other side of the earth. We gave up after a few minutes (digging is hard!), but with these books, I'm getting to reach your country... just in a different way than I had imagined.

Thank you so much for making **Diary of a Wimpy Kid** a success in your country. I hope you find the stories funny and that they inspire you to become writers and cartoonists. I feel very fortunate to have achieved my dream to become a cartoonist, and I hope you achieve your dream, too... whatever it might be.

I hope to one day visit China. It would be a dream come true!

I hope you enjoy the fifth **Wimpy Kid** book. Thank you again for embracing my books!

Jeff

有趣的书，好玩的书

夏 致

这是一个美国中学男生的日记。他为自己的瘦小个子而苦恼，老是会担心被同班的大块头欺负，会感慨"为什么分班不是按个头分而是按年龄分"。这是他心里一道小小的自卑，可是另一方面呢，他又为自己的脑瓜比别人灵光而沾沾自喜，心里嘲笑同班同学是笨蛋，老想投机取巧偷懒。

他在老妈的要求下写日记，幻想着自己成名后拿日记本应付蜂拥而至的记者；他特意在分班时装得不会念书，好让自己被分进基础班，打的主意是"尽可能降低别人对你的期望值，这样即使最后你可能几乎什么都不用干，也总能给他们带来惊喜"；他喜欢玩电子游戏，可是他爸爸常常把他赶出家去，好让他多活动一下。结果他跑到朋友家里去继续打游戏，然后在回家的路上用别人家的喷水器弄湿身子，扮成一身大汗的样子；他眼红自己的好朋友手受伤以后得到女生的百般呵护，就故意用绷带把自己的手掌缠得严严实实的装伤员，没招来女生的关注反而惹来自己不想搭理的人；不过，一山还有一山高，格雷再聪明，在家里还是敌不过哥哥罗德里克，还是被耍得团团转；而正在上幼儿园的弟弟曼尼可以"恃小卖小"，无论怎么捣蛋都有爸妈护着，让格雷无可奈何。

这个狡黠、机趣、自恋、胆小、爱出风头、喜欢懒散的男孩，一点都不符合人们心目中的那种懂事上进的好孩子形象，奇怪的是这个缺点不少的男孩子让我忍不住喜欢他。

人们总想对生活中的一切事情贴上个"好"或"坏"的标签。要是找不出它的实在可见的好处，它就一定是"坏"，是没有价值的。单纯的有趣，让我们增添几分好感和热爱，这难道不是比读书学习考试重要得多的事情吗?! 生活就像一个蜜糖罐子，我们是趴在桌子边踮高脚尖伸出手，眼巴巴地瞅着罐子的孩子。有趣不就是蜂蜜的滋味吗?

翻开这本书后，我每次笑声与下一次笑声之间停顿不超过五分钟。一是因为格雷满脑子的鬼主意和诡辩，实在让人忍俊不禁。二是因为我还能毫不费劲地明白他的想法，一下子就捕捉到格雷的逻辑好笑在哪里，然后会心一笑。

小学二年级的时候我和同班的男生打架;初一的时候放学后我在黑板上写"某某某（男生）是个大笨蛋";初二的时候，同桌的男生起立回答老师的提问，我偷偷移开他的椅子，让他的屁股结结实实地亲吻了地面……我对初中男生的记忆少得可怜。到了高中，进了一所重点中学，大多数的男生要么是专心学习的乖男孩，要么是个性飞扬的早熟少年。除了愚人节和邻班的同学集体调换教室糊弄老师以外，男生们很少再玩恶作剧了。仿佛大家不约而同都知道，自己已经过了有资格耍小聪明，并且耍完以后别人会觉得自己可爱的年龄了。

如果你是一位超过中学年龄的大朋友，欢迎你和我在阅读时光中做一次短暂的童年之旅;如果你是格雷的同龄人，我真羡慕你们，因为你们读了这本日记之后，还可以在自己的周围发现比格雷的经历更妙趣横生的小故事，让阅读的美好体验延续到生活里。

要是给我一个机会再过一次童年，我一定会睁大自己还没有患上近视的眼睛，仔细发掘身边有趣的小事情，拿起笔记录下来。亲爱的读者，不知道当你读完这本小书后，是否也有同样的感觉?

片刻之后我转念一想，也许从现在开始，还来得及呢。作者创作这本图画日记那年是 30 岁，那么说来我还有 9 年时间呢。

九 月

星期二

我就开门见山，直奔主题吧：这是一本日志，可不是什么日记①。我知道这个本子封面上印着什么，但我妈出门买本子的时候，我可是千叮咛万嘱咐，叫她别买写着"日记"二字的。

这下好了，就差没被一些个呆子碰上，要是被人看到我揣着这么个本子，肯定得闹误会了。还有一点我得赶紧澄清一下，那就是，我可没想写这玩意儿，这都是我妈的意思。

不过她要是以为我会拿这本子来记什么"心事"之类的，那就肯定是脑子进水了。所以啊，你也就别指望我会"亲爱的日记"来"亲爱的日记"去了。

我答应写这玩意的唯一理由是，我想到等我将来发达了，我可没时间整天回答记者们提出的愚蠢问题。到时候这书可就派上大用场了。

① 美国文化中，通常是女生在写日记（diary），且常以"亲爱的日记"（Dear Diary）开头。

1

正如我刚才所说，我总有一天会飞黄腾达，不过现在呢，我却身陷中学之中，周围还有一群白痴。

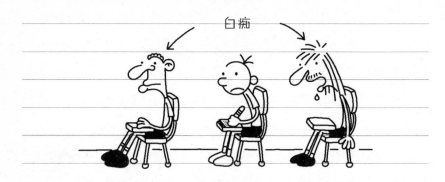

我要郑重声明——你们不妨录以备案，我认为中学是有史以来最木的发明。竟然把我这种还没到青春发育期的小孩跟那些一天得刮两次毛的"大猩猩"混在一起。

而且他们居然还对中学里的以大欺小问题现象大惑不解。

要我来说啊，年级应该按身高来划分，而不按年龄。不过这又有新麻烦了，要这样的话，我猜齐拉格·戈塔这类小屁孩就得一直呆在一年级了。

今天是开学第一天，我们大家都等着看老师匆匆跑进来，给我们安排座位。现在正是我在这本子上写写东西打发时间的好机会。

我顺道给你提个建议。开学第一天，你可千万要看清楚了才坐下。很可能你走进课室，随便找个破桌子，"砰"地把东西一股脑儿卸下来，这时老师就开口了：

所以以后凡上这一科，我就卡在克里斯·何塞和莱昂纳尔·詹姆斯之间，克里斯在前，莱昂纳尔在后。

杰森·布里尔来晚了，差点就要在我右边坐下，谢天谢地，好在我反应及时，在至关紧要的最后一刻阻止了这一灾难的发生。

下堂课①，我就该一进课室就赶紧抢到辣妹身边，在她们中间找位置坐下。不过我要是还这么干，就证明我去年的经验教训全白费了。

哥们儿，我真不知道最近女孩子都怎么了。小学那会儿可比现在简单多了。有一不成文的规定：只要跑步全班最快，便可尽

---

 ① 在美国，每次课都是学生换课室，而非固定课室换老师。

4

得女孩芳心。

而五年级时，我们班的飞毛腿是罗尼·麦克莱。

这年头可就复杂多了。现在就看你穿什么衣服啦，有没有钱啦，有没有翘臀啦之类的。罗尼这类跑步健将这会儿正不停挠头，不知所措呢。

我们年级目前最受欢迎的男生是布莱斯·安德森。我一直都跟女生打成一片，但布莱斯这家伙可是最近几年才出道的，真让人愤愤不平。

我至今还记得布莱斯小学时候的行径。

不过，当然了，现在老跟女生混在一起已经不吃香了。

前面说了，布莱斯是年级最红的男生，所以剩下来的男生只好在人气排行榜上争剩余的排名了。

我估计我今年的最佳排名也就在 52 和 53 之间了。 不过有一惊天喜讯——那就是我又能往上爬一位了，因为排我前面的查理·戴维斯下周就要箍牙去了。

我花了好大功夫来跟我哥们儿罗利（顺带一提，他的排名大概在 150 左右浮动）解释这个人气问题，不过，我猜他是左耳进右耳出了。

星期三

今天我们上体育课，我一出课室就马上溜到篮球场上，看看那块"千年奶酪"还在不在。 果不其然，它还呆在那儿。

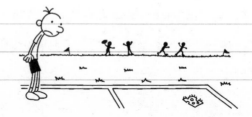

那块奶酪自开春以来就一直呆在那条柏油路上。我猜，那大概是有人吃三明治之类东西时掉下来的。再过了几天后，奶酪就开始发霉发臭了。之后再没有人去那块奶酪所在的篮球场打球了，尽管那是我们仅有的一个既有篮筐又有篮网的球场。

直到有一天，有个叫戴伦·沃尔什的小屁孩用手指头碰了一下那块奶酪，于是，所谓的"奶酪附体"宣告开始。这基本上类似于"警察抓小偷"，你要是被奶酪之手碰过了，就算是被"附体"了，除非你能找到下家，把霉运给传出去。

保护自己免受"奶酪附体"的唯一办法，就是食指搭在中指上作十字架状。但要一整天都时时刻刻记住保持手形，可实在不太容易。我最后干脆用透明胶把两个指头缠起来了，这样一来，它们就能一直保持交叉状。虽然我的书法课因此只拿了"差"，不过实在大有所值。

有个叫亚伯·霍尔的小屁孩自从四月份被奶酪之手碰过后，往后的八个月里几乎没人敢走近他。暑假的时候他搬家搬到了加利福尼亚，才把这"奶酪附体"一并带走了。

我只求没人再开始那"奶酪附体"了，因为我实在不想再担惊受怕了。

星期四

暑假结束了，我又得天天老早爬起来到学校上学去了，这个事实，真让我一时难以接受。

确切来说，我的暑假一开始就不爽，这还得要归功于我的哥哥罗德里克。

暑假开始没几天，有一天半夜，罗德里克把我从睡梦中叫醒。他说我已经沉睡了整整一个暑假，不过万幸的是我醒得正是时候，刚好赶上开学第一天。

你大概会说，这都中招，也太低能了吧。不过罗德里克当时整整齐齐地穿着校服，还调了我闹钟的时间，搞得真跟早上该出门了似的。还有，他把窗帘拉起来了，这样我就看不到外面一片漆黑了。

罗德里克把我叫醒之后，我就穿好衣服下楼，准备做点早餐吃，一如既往。

不过我猜我一定是闹出大的响动，因为没过多久，就看见老爸冲下楼冲我嚷嚷，说我凌晨3点吃麦片，闹得全家不安宁。

我花了足足一分钟才回过神来。

搞清楚来龙去脉后，我告诉老爸这是罗德里克耍的阴谋诡计，他才是罪魁祸首，该挨骂的是他，我是无辜的。

我一路跟着老爸下地下室，等着看他痛骂罗德里克。我实在等不及要看罗德里克遭报应。不过那家伙的掩饰手段实在高明。这下老爸反而认为是我神经不对头或思维短路之类的了。

<u>星期五</u>

今天上课时，老师给我们分了阅读小组。

他们并不会直接告诉你是被分到了尖子班还是基础班，不过你一看大家手里拿的书，心里就立刻明白了。

被分进尖子班，对我打击挺大的，因为这就表示我没法偷懒了。

去年年底他们筛选分班的时候，我费了好大功夫，力图确保今年能进基础班。

① *Bink Says Boo*，书名直译为《宾克说"布"》，"Boo"是小孩最容易发的音，因此可以断定这本书是给学龄前到低年级的孩子阅读的入门教程。

老妈跟校长关系很好，所以我猜肯定是她从中作梗，做了手脚，又把我弄回尖子班去了。

老妈总说我是聪明仔，不过是自己不肯"闪光"罢了。

话说我要是从罗德里克身上学到过什么的话，那就是学会了他那招：打消别人的任何期望，这样只需要做一丁点的小事——基本啥都没做，就能让人喜出望外。

其实我想混进基础班的阴谋没有得逞，我还是有点庆幸的。

我亲眼看到过一帮"开口说啪啪"的孩子们把书倒着拿，而且他们可不像是在开玩笑的样子。

星期六

好吧，第一周的学习总算过去了，今天我要睡个懒觉。

大多数的孩子都会选择在星期六早起，为了看卡通片，或者看什么都好，不过我是不会这么干的。我在周末起床的唯一理由，就是在床上呆久了，终于受不了自己的气味了。

不幸的是，老爸天天 6：00 起床，全不顾当天是星期几，也从来不考虑一下我想在周末放松放松——人之常情嘛。

今天也没什么可干的，所以我就跑罗利家去了。

罗利嘛，基本上算是我最要好的朋友了，但这个嘛，当然是要视情况而定了。

我从开学第一天起就躲着罗利，因为那天他真把我给惹毛了。

那天放学后我们在储物柜旁收拾好东西正准备走，罗利突然跑过来说——

想来我家玩玩么？

我都跟罗利说过无数次了，我们现在是中学生了，就不应该再说"玩"了，要说"混"。但是不管我敲他脑门多少次，他过后都总能忘得一干二净。

自从进了中学，我就开始注重保持形象了，但身边带着罗利，只会把形象搞砸。

我跟罗利认识好几年了。当时他刚搬来我家附近，他妈给他买了一本书——《到了新地方如何交朋友》，于是他就到我家门前来耍那些笨得不行的交友小伎俩。

　　我看我确实有点同情罗利，于是就决定：日后罩着这小·老弟吧。

　　有罗利在身边有时还真挺好，因为我总能把罗德里克耍我的花招通通用在罗利身上。

　　① 一个搭讪段子，用"Thermos"与"There must"谐音来开玩笑，典型的冷笑话。

星期一

　　还记得我说我平时怎么整罗利的么？哎，我有个弟弟叫曼尼，我在他身上搞恶作剧，从来没有过能全身而退的。

　　爸爸妈妈老护着他，当他是王子似的。不论他惹出多大乱子，他都能安安全全置身事外。

　　昨天，曼尼用那种擦不掉的彩笔在我卧室门上画了一幅自画像。我以为爸妈这回总该给他点颜色看看了，不过，一如既往，我又失算了。

最烦人的还是曼尼给我取的小名。他小的时候死活发不出"哥哥"这个音，于是就开始管我叫"波波①"。他到现在还这么叫我，我让爸妈纠正过他无数次了，但就是屡禁不止。

幸亏我的朋友们现在都还蒙在鼓里，真不容易，有好几次都险些穿帮。

① 英文中"Brother（哥哥）"和"Bubby（波波，俚语里指女性乳房）"押头韵，音近，所以曼尼说后者代替前者。

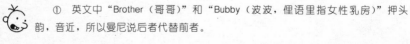

妈妈让我早上帮曼尼收拾东西准备上学。我一给他做好早餐，他就端着他的麦片，坐到他的痰盂上。

一到出门上托儿所的时候，他就起身，把没吃完的东西不管三七二十一全部倒到痰盂里。

妈妈老跟我发火，责备我吃不完早餐。不过她要是也尝尝每天早上刷痰盂刷出麦片来的味道，她也准保不会有胃口。

① 英文原文直译为："C"呢，就代表曲奇（Cookie），而曲奇呢，是给我吃的。

星期二

　　我不知道之前有没有跟你提起过，我可是个电玩高手。要是跟我们年级的人单挑，我敢说没人赢得了我。

　　可惜，老爸不懂得欣赏我这方面的技艺，他老是让我出门动一动。

　　晚饭过后，当老爸又开始唠叨让我出去户外活动活动的时候，我费了好半天劲跟他讲解电子游戏，苦口婆心跟他解释不必挨晒不必流汗，如何足不出户就能享受踢足球的乐趣。

　　不过，还是老样子，跟老爸讲逻辑就是讲不通。

　　老爸平时大体上还算机灵，不过一旦涉及常识问题，那可就说不准了。

我敢保证老爸一定会把我的游戏设备拆掉——要是他懂拆的话。万幸的是，这些设备一生产出来就是防摔防震防家长的。

　　每次老爸赶我出门做运动，我就跑到罗利家，在他家里照样玩我的游戏。

　　不幸的是，在罗利家我唯一能玩的就是赛车游戏之类的。

　　因为每次我带游戏去罗利家，他爸都会先上一些育儿网站检索，一旦查出游戏里含有打斗或暴力成分就一律免谈。

　　跟罗利玩一级方程式赛车特没劲，因为他可不像我这么敬

业．你只需要开赛之前给你的车子取一个恶搞的名字，你就能轻松赢他。

然后，当你的车超到他前头去的时候，他就彻底崩溃了。

反正我跟罗利一较高下之后，我就回家去了。进门之前在隔壁家的草坪洒水器边趟了几个来回，弄得好像一身大汗似的。只要略施小计就能混过老爸这关。

不过事与愿违，老妈一看到我湿成这样就责令我立即上楼洗澡。

我猜老爸一定是对昨天让我出门做户外活动感到非常满意，因为他今天又来了。

每次要玩游戏都得跑到罗利家去，真是让我烦透了。还有个叫弗雷格的怪人，就住在我家跟罗利家的中间，他还老喜欢在自家院子前转悠，实在没法不碰上他。

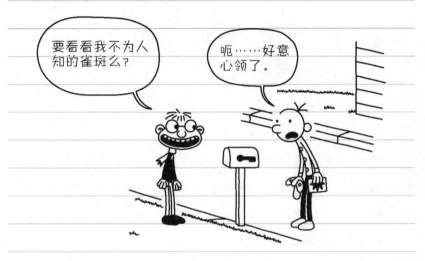

弗雷格跟我在同一个班上体育课，他的语言自成一家，比如说当他要去厕所的时候，他就说——

我们已经大致清楚弗雷格那套了，不过我看老师们大概还没弄懂。

今天，恐怕不用老爸赶，我自己也会到罗利家去了。因为哥哥罗德里克和他的乐队要在地下室里排演。他那个乐队实在让人不敢恭维，他们排练的时候，我实在没法在家里待下去。

他的乐队叫做"尿不湿"，不过他在小货车上写成了"水不湿①"。

你可能以为他写成这样是为了耍酷，不过我敢打赌，你要是跟他说"尿不湿"应该这么写，他的表情肯定就跟刚听到新闻一样。

 ① "尿不湿"取英文"Loaded Diaper"（用过的尿片）的意思。而罗德里克却拼写成了"Loded Diper"。

老爸不支持罗德里克组乐队，不过老妈举双手赞成。

罗德里克的第一套架子鼓，就是老妈给买的。

我看老妈大概是有这么个想法：让我们大家都去学乐器，好组建一个家庭乐队——就跟你在电视上看到的那样。

老爸非常厌恶重金属，而罗德里克和他的乐队玩的就是这种音乐。我看老妈倒不在乎罗德里克听什么音乐或玩什么风格，因为在她看来，音乐都一个样。今天早些时候，罗德里克在客厅里听 CD 的时候，老妈居然还跟着跳起舞来。

这搞得罗德里克周身不爽，所以他开着小货车去了趟商店，

15分钟后买了一副耳机回来，然后问题就圆满解决了。

星期四

昨天，罗德里克买了一张重金属摇滚CD，上面还贴着"家长警告"的标签。

我还从来没有听过值得标上"家长警告"的CD，因为爸妈向来不许我在商场买这种CD。看来我要是想听罗德里克的这张CD的话，在家里是绝对行不通的，唯一可行的办法就是神不知鬼不觉地将它带出家门。

今天一早，当罗德里克出门后，我就打电话让罗利把随身听带回学校。然后我就溜到罗德里克的房间，把这张碟从架上取走。

学校里是不准带随身听的，所以我们只能等到午休时分老师放我们出去的时候。时机一到，我跟罗利就赶紧溜到学校后院，把罗德里克的 CD 放进随身听。

天杀的罗利拿了随身听竟然忘记拿电池，所以我们是竹篮打水一场空。

还好我灵机一动，想到个玩法。

看谁能在最短时间内把耳机甩下来，就算谁赢，只准用头，不准用手。

我的最佳纪录是 7.5 秒，不过我感觉那次甩得都有点脑震荡了。

正玩到一半，克雷格老师从拐角处出现，把我们俩当场抓获。她从我手里没收了随身听，然后就开始唠唠唠唠数落我们。

不过我看她是误会了。她跟我们大谈摇滚乐何其"邪恶"，如何使我们的大脑致残等等。

我本想跟她讲随身听里面根本没有电池，不过看得出来，这时候打断她说话恐怕不太好。所以我就等啊等啊，等到她说完，我就说："是的，夫人。"

克雷格老师正打算放过我们，结果罗利却开始哭哭啼啼，说他害怕自己会变傻。

说实话，有时候我就是搞不懂那孩子。

星期五

这下可好，我自作自受，闯大祸了。

昨天半夜，大家都入睡之后，我悄悄下楼，跑到客厅打开音响听罗德里克的 CD。

我戴上罗德里克的新头戴式耳机，把音量开得巨大，然后按下"播放"键。

首先，我得说，这下我可彻底明白这 CD 为什么要贴 "家长警告" 的标签了。

可惜第一首歌才放了 30 多秒就被打断了。

我竟然没插耳机插头。结果音乐压根不是通过耳机出来的，而是通过喇叭直接放出来的。

老爸把我架回房间，转身把门关上，然后说——

　　每当老爸用那种语气说"哥们儿"的时候，我就知道麻烦来了。我头一次听老爸这么说"哥们儿"的时候，我没听出他是在说反话，结果就放松了警惕。

　　之后我可再也没上当了。

　　晚上老爸训了我十多分钟，然后我猜想他大概也觉得与其穿着内衣在我房里杵着，还不如回去睡觉。他罚我两周内不准玩电动游戏，我早就猜到了。 这就放过我了，我还是比较庆幸的。

老爸有个好处，就是发火之后，气消得也快，然后就没事了。通常如果你在他面前捣乱的话，他逮什么就冲你扔什么。

正确的捣乱时机：

错误的捣乱时机：

说起罚人，老妈的风格就大不一样。 要是你捣乱被她逮住，她首先会花若干天来考虑合适的量刑。

当你在等待被宣判的时候，你会尽力做点好事来希望博得减刑。

　　不过几天之后，正当你以为烟消云散、得意忘形之际，她就要过来宣判裁决了。

星期一

　　这个禁止玩游戏的惩罚比我想象中要麻烦得多。不过好在我还不是家里唯一一处在水深火热之中的人。

　　罗德里克最近也吃了老妈的苦头。曼尼搞到了一期罗德里克的《重金属》杂志，里面有一页比基尼女郎横躺在车盖上的照片。他居然拿了这张艳照去托儿所的"展示口语课"上展示。

我估计老妈接到托儿所老师的电话家访后很难高兴得起来。

我也看过那期杂志，凭良心说，我觉得这没什么大不了的。不过老妈对这种事情可绝不姑息。

对罗德里克的相应惩罚就是他得乖乖地回答老妈给他开出的系列问题。

这种杂志能让你进步么？

不能。

这种杂志能让你在学校更受欢迎么？

不能。

你现在怎么看待自己买这种杂志的行为？

我不是人。

买了这种不良杂志，你有什么话想对全体女士说？

我对不起女士们。

惩戒期还没过去，我还是不能玩电动游戏，所以曼尼就把我的游戏机给抢占了。老妈出去买了一大堆益智游戏给曼尼。我觉得看着他玩游戏，简直就是活受罪。

值得高兴的消息是我终于找到了一个突破罗利老爸安检的方法了。我只需把我的游戏光盘放在曼尼的《探索字母表》的盒子里就大功告成了。

① 原文中是 Three（三）跟 Tree（树）押韵。这里根据中文情况做了改译。

星期二

　　白天上课时，听说学生会竞选即将开始了。老实说，我对学生会从来不感冒。不过转念一想，我发现要是我能当选财政部长的话，那我在学校的气派可就大不一样了。

从来没人想竞选财政部长，因为大家都只关注大牌职位，比如学生会主席和副主席。所以我盘算着，只要我明天登记竞选，基本上这个财政部长的位置是非我莫属了，哇哈哈。

星期五

今天，我在竞选财政部长名单上写下了我的名字。不幸的是，一个叫马蒂·波特的小屁孩也觊觎财政部长一职，而且他在数学方面好像还挺行的。所以我立刻觉得情况有些不妙了。

我跟老爸说我要去竞选学生会职务，他听了相当激动。原来他在我这个年纪的时候也竞选过，而且还真让他当选了。

老爸在地下室里翻箱倒柜，找出了一张他当年的竞选海报。

正直
诚信
富于执行力

请投

秘书长候选人

弗兰克·赫夫利

　　我发现用海报来造势这个点子很不错，就让老爸开车带我去商场买了一堆物资。 我买了一大堆纸板和彩笔，一个晚上都在制作我的竞选宣传海报。 现在就盼着它们起作用了。

星期一

　　今天我把海报带回学校了，不能不承认，这些海报显得相当专业。

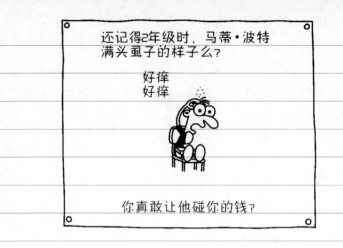

我一进学校就四处张贴我的海报。不过前后才挂了不到三分钟就让副校长罗伊给盯上了。

罗伊先生跟我说，不准给其他候选人造谣抹黑，我就告诉罗伊先生马蒂·波特长头虱的事情千真万确，而且闹得满城风雨，搞得学校几乎处于停课状态。

但他还是把我的海报全部揭了下来。所以今天当马蒂·波特四处派发棒棒糖来收买选票的时候，我的竞选海报却乖乖躺在副校长的垃圾桶里。我看我的政治生涯基本上就到此为止了。

十 月

星期一

终于到十月了，离万圣节只有30天之遥了。我特别喜欢过万圣节，尽管老妈说，我现在还去玩"不请客就捣乱"的把戏，是不是有点超龄了。

老爸也喜欢万圣节，不过原因跟我不同。万圣节之夜，当其他家长都在派发糖果的时候，老爸就抱着一大桶水躲在后院的灌木丛里。

一旦有青少年路过我们家的车道，老爸就把他们泼得浑身湿透。

我看老爸压根没理解万圣节的精髓。不过我可不打算去扫他的兴。

今晚是科罗斯兰高中鬼宅的首演之夜，我说服了老妈带我和罗利一起去。

罗利到我家的时候，居然穿了他去年的万圣节超人装。我早前给他打电话时还特意跟他说要穿正常点，不过这个他当然是不会听的了。

我尽量不让这傻事影响到我的情绪。老妈此前从不批准我去科罗斯兰鬼宅，现在好不容易能去，可不能让罗利把好事给搅黄了。罗德里克早就跟我说过这鬼屋，我盼星星盼月亮都盼了三年了。

不过刚到入口处的时候，我就开始有点想临阵脱逃了。

不过老妈看起来仿佛急于逛一圈了事，推着我们就一路进去了。过了大门之后，惊吓就一波接一波。吸血鬼突然现身，无头尸四处游弋，妖魔鬼怪层出不穷。不过最吓人的还是一个叫"断头巷"的地方，一个头戴曲棍球面具的大高个儿，开着一把货真价实的电锯朝着我们冲了过来。罗德里克说那电锯的刀刃是塑料的，不过我可不敢冒这个险。

嗡嗡嗡嗡嗡嗡嗡嗡嗡嗡！

就当电锯男快要追上我们的时候，老妈及时出来斡旋，救了我们一命。

太不像话了！

对不起，夫人。

老妈让电锯男给我们指明了出口，我们的鬼屋惊魂就到此结束了。我觉得老妈这么干让人挺难为情的，不过这次我很乐意网开一面，不予追究。

科罗斯兰鬼宅的事情让我想了又想。那些闹鬼的家伙收每人5美元的门票，而且人们排的长队足可以把科罗斯兰高中绕上半个圈。

我决定自己来搞一座鬼屋。当然啦，我非得拉上罗利一起干不可，因为老妈是不会同意我擅自把一楼改装成一个彻头彻尾的鬼屋的。

我知道罗利的老爸也不怎么看好这个点子，所以我们决定把鬼屋建在他们家的地下室，而且对他的父母暂时保密。

我跟罗利琢磨了一整天，想出了一个绝妙的鬼屋规划。

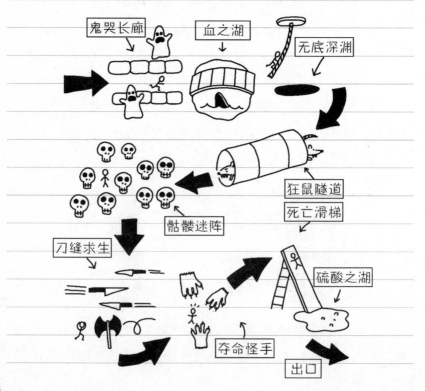

鬼哭长廊

血之湖

无底深渊

狂鼠隧道

死亡滑梯

骷髅迷阵

刀缝求生

硫酸之湖

夺命怪手

出口

我可不是在吹，我们的这个点子可比科罗斯兰高中鬼宅强太多了。

我们得先把风声放出去，好让大家知道我们的生意。所以我们买了纸张，做了一大叠传单。

我承认广告有点言过其实，不过为了确保当天有人来捧场，我们只好出此下策。

等我们在邻里周围派完传单，再回到罗利家的地下室的时候，都已经 2:30 了，而我们还压根没开始布置鬼屋呢。

所以我们临时决定从原计划中删除一些边角料。

3:00 一过，我们就到外头看看人来了没有。果不其然，已经有二十来个邻居家的孩子在罗利家地下室外排长队了。

就目前情况来看，虽然我们的传单上写着入场费为 50 美分，不过我们完全可以临时涨价赚它一票。

所以我就跟那些小·屁孩们说，实际入场费是 2 美元，50 美分是印刷错误。

第一个心不甘情不愿地掏出 2 美元的小·屁孩是谢恩·斯涅拉。他交了钱，我们就让他进去了，然后我就跟罗利在"鬼哭长廊"就位了。

"鬼哭长廊"其实就是一张床，我跟罗利一人一边。

我猜可能是我们把"鬼哭长廊"布置得稍微恐怖了一点，因为谢恩到了半路就不肯动了，在床底下蜷缩成一团。我们想尽办法

要让他爬出来，但他就是一动也不动。

我开始想，这小·屁孩要堵在这"鬼哭长廊"，那我们还做不做生意啊，这下亏死了，一定要把他给弄出来，得快！

最后，罗利的爸爸下楼了。看见他来我一开始还挺高兴的，想着他能帮我们把谢恩从床底下拖出来，这样我们的鬼屋好继续运作下去。不过罗利的老爸看起来更像是来添乱的。

用力戳，
用力戳

罗利的老爸盘问我们在干吗，还有谢恩为什么会蜷缩在床底。

我们就告诉他，这个地下室目前是鬼屋，谢恩其实是花钱请我们来吓他的。不过罗利的老爸不太买账。

我承认，只要你环顾四周，就会发现这房间看起来并不怎么阴森恐怖。时间有限，我们只布置了"鬼哭长廊"和"血之湖"——罗利的婴儿游泳池外加半瓶番茄酱。

我把我们的最初方案拿给罗利的老爸看，以便证明我们确实是在合法经营，不过他还是不予采信。

总而言之，我们的鬼屋就这么完了。

有点值得庆幸的是，罗利的爸爸不相信我们在做生意，所以也就没有让我们给谢恩退款。所以最后算下来，我们今天还净赚了2美元。

星期天

罗利因为昨天鬼屋闹出的乱子，被关禁闭了。一周不准看电视，而且期间不准我上他家去。

最后一条不太公平了，因为这根本是在惩罚我嘛，而我可是无辜的呀。 这下我要上哪去打游戏呢？

　　不过话说回来，我还是有点为罗利难过。 所以我决定今晚补偿他一下。 我开电视找到罗利平时爱看的节目，用电话给他做实况转播，这样他也能稍微感受一下。

喔！快看，那火焰喷射器多大啊！

啊，对，你看不到，不好意思。

　　我尽量紧跟画面加以解说，不过实话说，我不敢保证罗利是否能听出个所以然。

我敢打赌这部分一定很好玩。

哇哈哈！我猜对了真的很好玩

星期二

呼——，罗利的禁闭终于结束了，刚好赶上万圣节。我上他们家去看他的万圣节服装，说实话，我还真有点眼红。

罗利的妈妈给他买了一身骑士装，比他去年那套酷多了。

他那身骑士行头包括一个头盔、一个盾牌和一把货真价实的宝剑，应有尽有。

我还从来没有穿过商店里买来的套装呢。到现在我都没想好明晚要走什么风格，大概在最后一刻才东拼西凑仓促上路吧。我猜我可能又得来一次厕纸木乃伊的把戏了。

不过我看明晚很可能下雨，所以这恐怕不是最明智的选择。

过往几年里，附近的大人们看我一身的蹩脚装扮都快抓狂了，我简直开始怀疑他们是看在这身蹩脚服装的分上才多给我几把糖的。

　　不过我真的没时间来精心制作万圣节装束，因为我还要负责设计明晚我跟罗利的最佳出行路线。

　　今年我有一个计划，准能挣到比去年多一倍的糖果。

万圣节

　　离挨家挨户闹"不请客就捣乱"的出发时间仅剩半个小时了，但我还是没整出一套万圣节装束。当时我真想干脆继续去年的装束，把牛仔进行到底算了。

　　不过就在这个时候，老妈敲开我的门，递给我一套海盗装、一个眼罩，还有一个钩子什么的。

　　罗利6：30左右穿着他的骑士装出现了，不过这身骑士套装跟昨天看到的那套比起来简直有天壤之别。

　　罗利的妈妈给他的套装增添了一些防护设施，这样一来，他的这身衣服就让人完全莫名其妙了。

　　她给罗利的头盔上凿了个大洞，以防他看不见路，在他的盔甲上贴满了反光胶布，又让他里面穿棉袄，裹得严严实实的，还把他的宝剑换成了荧光棒。

　　我一把抓起我的枕头套，正准备跟罗利出门，就被老妈拦截了下来。

好家伙，我就知道老妈给我买海盗装肯定另有企图。

我跟她说我们绝对没法带上曼尼一起走，因为我们要在三小时内突袭 152 户人家。而且我们还会经过巨蟒大道，太危险了，非常不适合曼尼这样的小家伙。

我实在不该提及后面那部分的，因为紧接着就看到老妈把老爸叫出来，让他一路保驾护航并确保我们一步都不踏出我们的街区。老爸使劲想摆脱这差事，不过老妈一旦打定主意，就谁都没有办法改变了。

我们还没走出自家的车道就碰上了邻居米切尔先生和他们家小·孩杰瑞米。自然而然地，队伍就又添了两名冗员。

每逢碰上装饰得比较诡异的房子，曼尼和杰瑞米就不肯去玩"不请客就捣乱"，仅这一条就基本排除了我们街区的所有房子。

老爸和米切尔先生开始聊起足球什么的，每当其中一方要大发议论的时候，他们就在半路停下来。

叭啦 叭啦 叭啦 叭啦 叭啦 叭啦 叭啦

叭啦 叭啦 叭啦 叭啦 叭啦 叭啦 叭啦

所以我们基本上从一家走到另一家都得花上 20 多分钟。

几个小·时后，老爸和米切尔先生就各自带着小·家伙回家了。

我太高兴了，因为这表示我和罗利可以独立干大事了。我的枕头套里还空空如也，所以我要抓紧时间，弥补回来。

过了一会儿，罗利跟我说他要"嘘嘘"。我让他再憋 45 分钟。不过当我们走到奶奶家门前时，看情形如果不让罗利去方便一下的话就得出大乱子了。

我跟罗利说，他要是不能在一分钟之内解决，我就要开吃——

他的糖了。

之后我们又继续踏上征途。不过已经 10：30 了，我猜这个时候恐怕多数成年人都认为万圣节已经圆满结束了。

这个是看得出来的，因为从这个时候开始，他们过来开门时就多半都穿着睡衣了，还对你投以怨毒的目光。

我们决定打道回府了。老爸和曼尼走了之后，我们加快进度，挽回了不少损失。要到了这么多糖果，我还是十分满意的。

回家还没走到半路，就看到一辆皮卡沿着大街一路咆哮过来，车上全是高中生。

坐在卡车后面的那个小屁孩拿着个灭火器，当车开过我们身边的时候，他就朝我们开火了。

喷 喷！

我得好好儿赞誉一下罗利的功勋，因为他凭着一个盾牌为我们挡住了几乎95％的水。要不是他这么英勇，我们的糖果恐怕都得泡汤了。

卡车开过之后，我冲他们大喊了一句，不过还没过2秒钟我就开始后悔了。

卡车司机猛一刹车就掉头朝我们开过来了，我跟罗利撒腿就跑，那帮家伙紧随其后。

我唯一能想到的安全避难所就是奶奶家，我们横穿几个后院走捷径抢到了奶奶家。奶奶这会儿早就睡了，不过我知道她在门廊的毯子下面会藏一把备用钥匙。

一进去，我就透过窗子看他们有没有追过来，一点不错，他们追得很紧。我费尽心思想把他们骗走，不过他们就是一动都不动。

　　过了一会儿，我发现这帮小·青年跟我们耗上了，非要把我们等出来不可，所以我们决定干脆就在奶奶家过夜了。这下就有恃无恐了，我们开始嚣张起来，学猴子乱叫，嘲弄他们。

　　好吧，至少我知道我是在学猴子叫，至于罗利在学什么叫——大概是学猫头鹰吧，反正我看也差不多。

　　我给老妈打了电话，跟她说我们今晚就在奶奶家过夜了。不过老妈在电话那头听起来怒不可遏。

　　她说现在可不是假期，明天还要上学，马上给我回家。这就意味着：我们得开始逃难了。

我看了看窗外，这次没看到那辆卡车了，不过我估计这帮家伙正暗地里埋伏着，为了要诱使我们出来。

我们从后门溜出来，越过奶奶家的栅栏，一路朝巨蟒大道狂奔。我知道我们朝那边跑生还的概率较大，因为那里没有街灯。

巨蟒大道本来就够可怕了，更何况还有一车的小青年在围追堵截。每次看到有车来，我们就赶紧伏到灌木丛里。步履维艰，半个小时还走不到 100 米。

真是难以置信，我们一路有惊无险，终于安全到家。一直走到自家门外的车道，我们俩才敢放松警惕。

就在这时，只听见一阵巨响，然后就看到一团巨浪朝我们袭来。

天哪，我把老爸这手给忘了，这下可付出了沉痛的代价。

我跟罗利进家门的时候，我们把糖全都掏出来晾在餐桌上。

搜救过程中，唯一幸存的，就是一些玻璃纸包着的薄荷糖和加里森博士送给我们的护齿牙刷。

我看下次万圣节我干脆就呆在家里不出门了，就跟老妈磨蹭，哀求她把搁在冰箱上面的雀巢花生巧克力给我几块算了。

十一月

星期四

今天坐校巴上学经过奶奶家时，看到她的房子被厕纸缠得一塌糊涂，我并不感到特别意外。

不过我还是稍微有一点点自责的，因为看样子要花好长一段时间才能把它搞干净了。不过从好的方面来说，奶奶已经退休了，说不定她赋闲在家今天刚好找不到事儿干呢。

星期三

第三堂课，体育老师安德伍德先生宣布：接下来男生要上长达六周的摔跤课。

要是说有一样东西绝大多数男生都感兴趣的话，那就是职业摔跤了。安德伍德先生的话就跟引爆了一颗重磅炸弹一样。

体育课一下课就到了午饭时分，饭堂里乱成一团，活像疯人院一样。

　　搞摔跤集训，我真不知道学校是怎么想的。

　　不过我打定主意，要是我还想活过这一个半月，不被别人拧成麻花的话，我还是在摔跤上做点功课为妙。

　　所以我就租了一堆游戏来学习摔跤手法。你猜怎么着？才不到一会儿，我就摸到窍门了。

说实在的，班上的其他同学最好打醒十二分精神了，因为我要是继续这么练下去的话，足以对他们构成极大威胁。

还有，我不能锋芒太露。看吧，这个叫皮里斯顿·玛德的小屁孩因为在篮球队里表现最为出色而获得了本月体育之星的称号，照片就被人贴到走廊上了。

每当有人大喊这个名字的时候，大家都得花上足足 5 秒才能

想起"皮·玛德"的标准读音。这么一喊开来，皮里斯顿就彻底
毁了。

星期四

　　我发现今天上课安德伍德先生教的摔跤跟电视上那种完全不
是一回事。

　　首先，我们得穿一种叫"背心"的东西，看起来就跟80年代
人们穿的那种游泳衣似的。

　①　原文"Pee（尿）"与"P."谐音，Mud（泥巴）与Mudd（玛德）谐音，这
里迁就汉语加以改译。

其次，摔跤时候不准用"旱地拔葱"这种招式，也不许拿椅子打别人的头，这些招式统统都不准用。

而且连四周带护栏的摔跤场都没有，只有一张闻上去满是汗臭，就跟从来没洗过一样的垫子。

安德伍德先生开始邀请志愿者上来配合示范"锁臂摔跤"的手法，他可千万别指望我会举手响应。

我跟罗利尽量往体操馆的后边靠近帘子的角落躲，不过女生正好在帘子后面练体操。

呵呵呵！

我们赶紧离开是非之地，回到男生队伍的后面。

安德伍德先生还是把我挑了出来，大概是因为我是班里最轻的男生，他可以毫不费力就把我颠来倒去。他给大家示范了如何"单臂扼颈"、"反抱"和"技术放倒"之类的。

当他示范"背负式摔击"的动作时，我感到身上一阵凉意，我看大概是我的背心没把身子包住，大有走光之意。

真是吉星高照，幸好女孩子都在体操馆的另一头。

安德伍德先生把大家按体重分了组，我一开始还倍感高兴，因为这就表示我不用跟班尼·威尔斯那种家伙摔跤了，那家伙能推举得动足足250磅的重量啊。

可是当我知道谁来当我的对手时，我马上就改变主意了，我宁可选班尼·威尔斯。

弗雷格是唯一的轻得足以跟我放在同一个重量级的小家伙。很明显当安德伍德先生指导技法的时候，弗雷格一定听得很用心，因为他次次都能把我摔倒。整个第七节课我就这么跟弗雷格打交道，我从来都没想过要跟他混这么熟。

星期二

这个摔跤课可真是把我们学校闹翻了天。现在这帮小屁孩在走廊也摔跤，在课室也摔跤，逮哪儿摔哪儿。情形最惨烈的还要数午饭后的 15 分钟休息时间。

简直没法安生走路了，每走几步路都会碰上这些扭成一团的小家伙。所以我就尽量跟他们保持安全距离。你看着吧，这里面说不定就有一个傻瓜会滚到那"千年奶酪"上面，然后再掀"奶酪附体"的血雨腥风。

　　还有一大问题就是我每天都得跟弗雷格摔跤。 不过今早我忽然灵光一闪，我要是能脱离弗雷格的重量级的话，我就不用再跟他摔跤了。

　　所以今天我在背心底下塞了一堆袜子和衣物，以便增重进入下一个重量级。

　　不过我体重还是太轻，升级无望。

我这下才明白我非得实打实地增肥不可。一开始我打算狂吃垃圾食品，不过后来我想出了一个更好的点子。

我决定增加肌肉而不是增加脂肪。

我之前对健身从不感兴趣，不过这个摔跤课让我开始重新反思了。

我发现要是能练就一身肌肉，将来迟早会管用的。

开春就要上橄榄球课了，到时候球员就会被分成"布衣"和"皮衣"①两队。而我一般都被分到"皮衣"队。

我觉得他们这么干就是故意让身材不好的男生自惭形秽。

我要是能来几块肌肉的话，明年四月就大为可观了。

① 原文"Shirts（衬衫）and skins（皮肤）"指的是一组穿上衣，另一组光膀子，这里戏作"皮衣"。

今天晚餐后，我把老爸跟老妈召集起来，跟他们讲了我的大计。我跟他们说我需要些高强度训练器械和一些增重粉①。

我给他们看了一些我在商店买的健美杂志，好让他们知道我有多么狂热。

老妈一开始没怎么表态，不过老爸显得相当热心。大概是因为他见我回心转意而备感欣慰吧，我小时候可不这样——

① 增重粉（Weight-gain powder）是一种全面增长体重的复合剂，主要成分包括碳水化合物、蛋白质、各种维生素和微量元素，可快速增加体重。

老妈说，我要是想要一套健身设备的话，就得先证明我有坚持按时锻炼的决心。 她说我要是能把仰卧起坐和开合跳[①]坚持两周她就相信我。

我不得不跟她解释，要是想要全面健身的话，一套健身房的高科技器材是必不可少的，不过老妈不吃这套。

老爸说我要是真想来一套卧推杠铃的话，就食指搭在中指上[②]求神保佑，盼着圣诞节到来吧。

① Jumping Jack，开合跳，又叫跳爆竹。
② Keep fingers crossed，如同前面说过的防护 "奶酪附体" 的办法，即食指搭在中指上作十字架状以祈福。

可是圣诞节还有一个半月才到呢。而且我要是再让弗雷格把我摔倒的话，我的精神就要彻底崩溃了。

看起来老爸老妈是见死不救了。这就表示我得亲自出马了，历来如此。

星期六

我实在等不及了，今天就要实施我负重锻炼的大计。虽然老妈不给我买器材，但我是决不会让这件事拖我后腿的。

我跑去把冰箱里的牛奶和橙汁的罐子倒空，往里头灌满沙子，然后把它们分别固定在扫帚柄的两头，就这样做好了一副相当不错的杠铃。

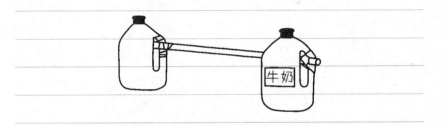

然后我又拿烫衣板和几个盒子做了个简易卧推架。万事俱备之后，我就要正式开始我的举重训练了。

我还需要一个练习搭档，所以就叫上了罗利。可是当我看到他穿得怪模怪样出现在我家门口时，我就知道邀他过来真是犯了个大错。

　　我让罗利先来举，主要是因为我想先观望一下，看看这个扫帚柄是否经得起考验。

　　他才举了五下就要撒手不干了，这我可不能答应——有个练习搭档就是好，可以时刻鞭策你，好让你超越极限。

再来15个！好样的！

　　我就知道罗利对待举重的态度不够端正，不像我这么投入，所以我决定做个实验，看看他到底有多专注。

　　趁罗利一套卧推动作还没举完，我跑进去从罗德里克垃圾堆成山的抽屉里翻出了一个假鼻子和一撮小·胡子。

当罗利放下杠铃正准备再举起来的时候，我俯下身去朝他看了一眼。

毫无疑问，罗利已经完全魂飞魄散了。他甚至都没力气把杠铃从胸口再托起来了。我本想去帮帮他的，不过我认为，如果不让罗利自己意识到问题的严重，他是永远无法赶上我的思想觉悟的。

不过我最后还是得出手搭救了，因为他居然出此下策：想把牛奶罐子咬破好让沙子漏出来。

罗利从卧推架上下来后，就到我来举了。不过罗利说他感觉不太舒服呆不下去，就匆匆回家了。

你看嘛，我就知道他这人准会让事情泡汤。你实在不能指望别人能跟你有同样程度的热忱。

星期三

今天地理课上小测验，实话说，我等这天等了好久了。

测验内容是写美国各州州政府所在地的名称，我坐在课室后面，旁边刚好就有一张巨幅美国地图。而且所有州政府的地名都是用红色印的，所以我觉得这次测验基本就可以高枕无忧了。

正当考试快要开始的那一刻，坐在课室前面的芭迪·法雷尔突然大呼小叫。

老师！老师！

芭迪告诉艾拉老师，说在小测验之前应该先把美国地图给遮起来。

多亏了芭迪的高风亮节，我的这次测验挂掉了。有朝一日，我一定要报这一箭之仇。

星期四

晚上老妈来到我的房间，手里拿着一张海报。一看到这海报，我心里就完全明白怎么回事了。

那是一个告示，大意就是说学校秋季戏剧会演要找小演员试镜。天哪，我在餐桌上看到这海报的时候就该把它顺手扔了。

我苦苦哀求，让老妈不要逼我报名。学校的戏剧会演通常都是音乐剧，而我这辈子最不愿意干的事情就是当着全校的面独唱了。

不过我无助的哀求似乎让老妈更坚定了她让我报名的决心。

老妈说，小孩子要全面发展就得尝试不同的事物。

老爸闻声赶来我的房间里，看看是怎么回事。我跟他说老妈让我报名演出，不过我要是去演出排练的话，那我的健身计划就彻底完蛋了。

我就知道老爸会站在我这边。不过老爸跟老妈才争执了几分钟就败下阵来。老爸哪里是老妈的对手呢？

这也就是说，我明天就得去为这个学校的戏剧会演试镜了。

星期五

今天要上演的剧目是《绿野仙踪》。一大堆孩子穿着各色戏装前来试镜。

我还没看过这部电影，所以现在感觉就像走在一场怪物巡游中，跟活见鬼一样。

我们的音乐总监诺顿太太让大家都来唱《亚美利加》①，以便听辨我们的歌喉。我跟一群男孩一起试唱，他们也是被老妈弄过来的。我尽量压低声音，唱得细不可闻，不过还是没能幸免，被挑出来了。

多甜美的男高②啊！

① 《My Country' Tis of Thee》也称为《America》，是一首美国爱国歌曲，歌词是由山缪·弗朗西斯·史密斯（Samuel Francis Smith）所作，而曲调则与英国国歌《天佑吾王》相同，是美国在 19 世纪时所使用的国歌。

② Soprano，童声男高音。

我不知道"男高"是什么东西，不过从女生的咯咯窃笑看来，我猜它就不是什么好东西。

　　试镜就这么没完没了地进行着。最后一场是试听桃乐丝的唱段，我估计桃乐丝大概是什么主角之类的。

　　第一个来试演桃乐丝的，除了那个芭迪还能有谁。

　　这一来，我倒想试试看争取演巫师那个角色了，因为我听说在戏里面，那巫师对桃乐丝百般迫害，丧尽天良。

　　不过后来有人告诉我，巫师有两个，一个好的，一个坏的。就我的运气来看，搞不好会被选为好巫师，那就没劲了。

星期一

　　我还指望诺顿太太能把我从剧中剔出去呢，不过今天她宣布人人有份。不知走了什么运了。

　　诺顿太太给大家放了《绿野仙踪》的电影以便大家了解剧情。我一直在盘算着演什么角色比较好，不过基本上每个角色都得或多或少地唱唱跳跳。不过电影放到一半，我忽然灵机一动，找到我的理想角色了。 我要报名扮演大树，因为：一、他们不用唱歌；二、他们有一场拿苹果来砸桃乐丝的戏。

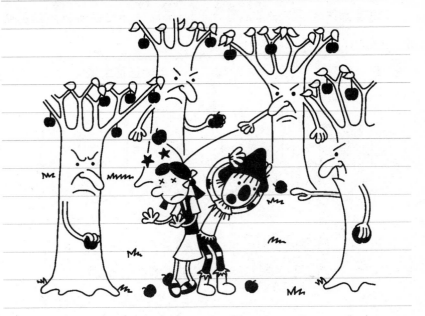

在现场观众的众目睽睽之下拿苹果来扔芭迪·法雷尔简直就像是美梦一样。 要真能这样，事成之后我还要谢谢老妈呢。

电影结束后，我就报名扮演大树。 不幸的是，还有另一堆家伙跟我有同样的想法，所以我猜有不少人和我一样跟芭迪有过节。

星期三

正如老妈说的，许愿的时候可得小心事与愿违。 我入选大树的角色了，不过却不知是喜是悲。 大树的戏服上没有挖洞让人把手伸出来，所以我看扔苹果的想法基本就没戏了。

　　我这角色还能有句台词，我真该感到庆幸了。因为太多孩子来试镜了，角色不够，他们只好杜撰新的角色出来。

　　罗德尼·詹姆斯本来想扮演铁皮人的，结果却只得扮演一棵矮灌木。

星期五

　　记得我说过我还挺走运，捡了个有台词的角色么？好吧，今天我才发现我在全剧中只有一句台词。是在桃乐丝从我的树枝上摘苹果时讲的。

　　也就是说，我每天排练两个小时就是为了说这么一句傻了吧唧的台词。

　　我开始觉得还是像罗德尼·詹姆斯扮演矮灌木这样比较爽。他找了个法儿把游戏机藏到戏服里了，打游戏来消磨时间可比干站着好多了。

　　我又开始想方设法让诺顿太太把我开掉了。 不过如果你的台词只有一个字，你实在没有发挥的余地来把戏搞砸。

星期四

　　戏剧还有几天就要上演了，不过我目前还没看到这出戏有一丝圆满成功的希望。

　　首先是没人肯花工夫去背台词，不过这都要怪诺顿太太。

　　排练期间，诺顿太太在舞台侧边小小声地给每个演员提醒台词。

　　不敢想象下周二，当诺顿太太坐在 10 米开外的钢琴旁弹伴奏的时候，这戏要怎么演下去。

　　还有一件特别糟糕的事情，那就是诺顿太太不断加场景添角色。

　　昨天，她把这个一年级的小屁孩加进来，扮演桃乐丝的小狗托托。不过今天这小屁孩的妈妈找上门来，嚷着要让她的小孩直立行走，因为四足着地爬来爬去实在太"掉价"了。

所以现在我们的剧中就有了一只整场戏都只用后足站立行走的狗了。

不过诺顿太太最大的败笔是她亲自写了歌让我们这些大树来唱。她说戏中的每一个角色都应该享有放声歌唱的机会。

今天我们就花了一个小时来学这首有史以来写得最烂的歌。

我们三棵树……

谢天谢地，罗德里克应该不会过来看我出丑了。因为诺顿太太说这个演出会安排在一个"半正式场合"，而罗德里克是断不会为了看一个中学生演的戏而大费周章去打领带的。

不过今天也并非全无好事。就在排练快要结束的时候，亚奇·凯利被罗德尼·詹姆斯给绊了一跤，却苦于没法伸手撑地，硬生生摔下来，把牙给磕坏了。

所以有一空前利好消息，那就是他们允许我们这些大树凿个洞把手伸出来了。

星期二

今晚学校的大作《绿野仙踪》就要上演了。在开演之前我就看到了不祥的征兆。

当我透过幕布来偷看有多少来宾的时候，你猜我见到谁了？我的哥哥罗德里克！他就正好在我跟前，还打着方便领带。

他肯定是知道我今晚要开口唱，

所以不肯放过看我出洋相的机会。

原定计划是 8:00 开演的，不过罗德尼·詹姆斯怯场，结果推迟了好一阵。

你会发现连那些杵在台上发呆的跑龙套的也能把戏搞砸。 罗德尼就是死活不肯动，最后只好由他妈妈把他带走了。

到了 8:30 左右戏才正式开演。 果然不出我所料，没人能记住自己的台词，不过大家跟着诺顿太太的钢琴走，戏演得还算顺畅。

那个扮演小·狗托托的小·屁孩搬了个小板凳过来还带了一叠漫画书上台看，彻底破坏了小·狗原来的形象。

到了森林那场的时候，我和其他大树赶紧走位。幕布升了起来，升到尽头的时候，我听到了曼尼的声音。

这下可好。我掩盖了 5 年的绰号，这下要在众目睽睽之下彻底败露了。我感觉到 300 双眼睛朝我看过来。

所以我就即兴发挥了一下，把这尴尬转嫁给亚奇·凯利了。

但是更大的糗事还没过去。当我听到诺顿太太开始弹"我们三棵树"伴奏的前几小节时，我的胃就不安宁。

我向观众席望过去，发现罗德里克正端着摄像机。

我知道我要是唱了这歌，还让罗德里克给拍了下来，他一定会永久珍藏这个影带，并随时拿出来取笑我，这样我一辈子不得安宁了。

我不知如何是好，所以当需要开唱的时候，我就默不做声。

头几秒钟还没什么问题。我打定主意，只要我基本不唱，罗德里克就没什么可以要挟我的。不过几秒钟过后，另外两棵树察觉出了我的异样：我压根没唱。

我猜他们大概以为我发现了状况而他们还浑然不知，所以他们的声音也越来越小，最后干脆也停下不唱了。

这下我们三个人都默默站在台上，一个字都不唱了。诺顿太太以为我们忘词了，所以走到台边给我们小声提示歌词。

这歌本来不超过3分钟，不过我现在却觉得这比一个半小时还漫长。我只盼幕布快点降下来，这样我们好赶紧逃离舞台。

就在这时我瞥见芭迪·法雷尔在舞台侧面怒目而视，要是眼神能杀人的话，连树都要被她杀死了。她大概怨我们害得她跻身百老汇的星梦难圆了。

看到她站在那儿，我就想起了我当初报名扮演大树的最初动机。

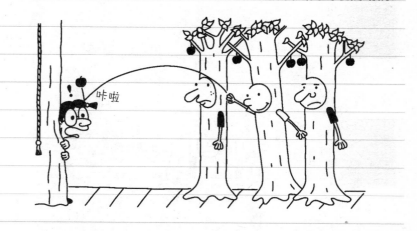

卡啦

很快，其他两棵树也开始捡苹果扔她了。我记得连托托也加入到我们的行列了。

不知道谁把她的眼镜给砸掉了，还碎了一块镜片。诺顿太太只好紧急叫停。之后就没法开演了，因为芭迪脱了眼镜后两眼一摸瞎，连半米远的东西都看不见。

演出结束后，我们就全家一起回去了。老妈原本带了一束花过来，而且我估计这花本来是要献给我的，不过最后被她直接扔进门口垃圾筒里了。我只希望来看戏的人都像我一样乐在其中，呵，那我就心满意足了。

TO MOM, DAD, RE, SCOTT, AND PATRICK

DIARY
of a
Wimpy Kid

$$\textcircled{1}$$

by Jeff Kinney

SEPTEMBER

<u>Tuesday</u>

First of all, let me get something straight: This is a JOURNAL, not a diary. I know what it says on the cover, but when Mom went out to buy this thing I SPECIFICALLY told her to get one that didn't say "diary" on it.

Great. All I need is for some jerk to catch me carrying this book around and get the wrong idea.

The other thing I want to clear up right away is that this was MOM's idea, not mine.

But if she thinks I'm going to write down my "feelings" in here or whatever, she's crazy. So just don't expect me to be all "Dear Diary" this and "Dear Diary" that.

The only reason I agreed to do this at all is because I figure later on when I'm rich and famous, I'll have better things to do than answer people's stupid questions all day long. So this book is gonna come in handy*.

* come in hardy
派上用场

Like I said, I'll be famous one day, but for now I'm stuck in middle school with a bunch of morons.

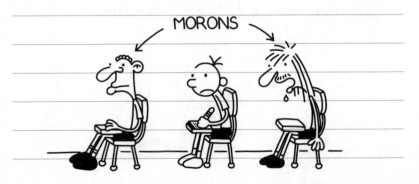

Let me just say for the record that I think middle school is the dumbest idea ever invented. You got kids like me who haven't hit their growth spurt* yet mixed in with these gorillas who need to shave twice a day.

* growth spurt
生长突增期

And then they wonder why bullying is such a big problem in middle school.

If it was up to me, grade levels would be based on height, not age. But then again, I guess that would mean kids like Chirag Gupta would still be in the first grade.

Today is the first day of school, and right now we're just waiting around for the teacher to hurry up and finish the seating chart. So I figured I might as well write in this book to pass the time.

By the way, let me give you some good advice. On the first day of school, you got to be real careful where you sit. You walk into the classroom and just plunk your stuff down on any old desk and the next thing you know the teacher is saying—

I HOPE YOU ALL LIKE WHERE YOU'RE SITTING, BECAUSE THESE ARE YOUR PERMANENT SEATS.

GAAH!

So in this class, I got stuck with Chris Hosey in front of me and Lionel James in back of me.

Jason Brill came in late and almost sat to my right, but luckily I stopped that from happening at the last second.

Next period, I should just sit in the middle of a bunch of hot girls as soon as I step in the room. But I guess if I do that, it just proves I didn't learn anything from last year.

Man, I don't know WHAT is up with girls these days. It used to be a whole lot simpler back in elementary school. The deal was, if you were the fastest runner in your class, you got all the girls.

And in the fifth grade, the fastest runner was Ronnie McCoy.

Nowadays, it's a whole lot more complicated. Now it's about the kind of clothes you wear or how rich you are or if you have a cute butt or whatever. And kids like Ronnie McCoy are scratching their heads wondering what the heck* happened.

* heck是hell 的弯婉用 法 , what the heck意 为"搞什么 嘛",表示 迷惑、诧 异、懊恼 等。

The most popular boy in my grade is Bryce Anderson. The thing that really stinks is that I have ALWAYS been into girls, but kids like Bryce have only come around in the last couple of years.

I remember how Bryce used to act back in elementary school.

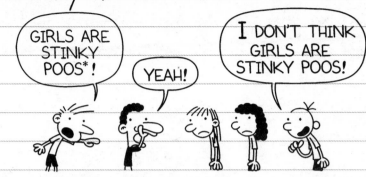

* poos
大便

But of course now I don't get any credit for sticking with the girls all this time.

Like I said, Bryce is the most popular kid in our grade, so that leaves all the rest of us guys scrambling for the other spots.

The best I can figure is that I'm somewhere around 52nd or 53rd most popular this year. But the good news is that I'm about to move up one spot because Charlie Davies is above me, and he's getting his braces next week.

I try to explain all this popularity stuff to my friend Rowley (who is probably hovering right around the 150 mark, by the way), but I think it just goes in one ear and out the other with him.

Wednesday

Today we had Phys Ed, so the first thing I did when I got outside was sneak off to the basketball court to see if the Cheese was still there. And sure enough, it was.

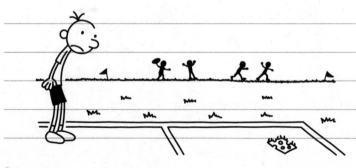

That piece of Cheese has been sitting on the blacktop since last spring. I guess it must've dropped out of someone's sandwich or something. After a couple of days, the Cheese started getting all moldy and nasty. Nobody would play basketball on the court where the Cheese was, even though that was the only court that had a hoop with a net.

Then one day, this kid named Darren Walsh touched the Cheese with his finger, and that's what started this thing called the Cheese Touch. It's basically like the Cooties*. If you get the Cheese Touch, you're stuck with it until you pass it on to someone else.

SCREAM!

The only way to protect yourself from the Cheese Touch is to cross your fingers.

But it's not that easy remembering to keep your fingers crossed every moment of the day. I ended up taping mine together so they'd stay crossed all the time. I got a D in handwriting, but it was totally worth it.

This one kid named Abe Hall got the Cheese Touch in April, and nobody would even come near him for the rest of the year. This summer Abe moved away to California and took the Cheese Touch with him.

I just hope someone doesn't start the Cheese Touch up again, because I don't need that kind of stress in my life anymore.

<u>Thursday</u>
I'm having a seriously hard time getting used to the fact that summer is over and I have to get out of bed every morning to go to school.

My summer did not exactly get off to a great start, thanks to my older brother Rodrick.

100

A couple of days into summer vacation, Rodrick woke me up in the middle of the night. He told me I slept through the whole summer, but that luckily I woke up just in time for the first day of school.

* shoot
可恶（通常是女士用词，是有教养的一种说法）

You might think I was pretty dumb for falling for that one, but Rodrick was dressed up in his school clothes and he set my alarm clock ahead to make it look like it was the morning. Plus, he closed my curtains so I couldn't see that it was still dark out.

After Rodrick woke me up, I just got dressed and went downstairs to make myself some breakfast, like I do every morning on a school day.

But I guess I must have made a pretty big racket* because the next thing I knew, Dad was downstairs, yelling at me for eating Cheerios* at 3:00 in the morning.

* make big racket
大声喧哗
* Cheerios
美国一种历史悠久的早餐麦片品牌

It took me a minute to figure out what the heck was going on.

After I did, I told Dad that Rodrick had played a trick on me, and HE was the one that should be getting yelled at.

Dad walked down to the basement to chew Rodrick out, and I tagged along. I couldn't wait to see Rodrick get what was coming to him.

But Rodrick covered up his tracks pretty good. And to this day, I'm sure Dad thinks I've got a screw loose* or something.

* have a screw loose 一般用来形容某人脑子有问题

Friday
Today at school we got assigned to reading groups.

They don't come right out and tell you if you're in the Gifted group or the Easy group, but you can figure it out right away by looking at the covers of the books they hand out.

I was pretty disappointed to find out I got put in the Gifted group, because that just means a lot of extra work.

When they did the screening at the end of last year, I did my best to make sure I got put in the Easy group this year.

FRED PICKED UP THE BUH... BAH... BEE...

THE "BOOK."

WHEW. THANKS!

* tight
with...
和某人关系
密切

Mom is real tight with* our principal, so I'll bet she stepped in and made sure I got put in the Gifted group again.

Mom is always saying I'm a smart kid, but that I just don't "apply" myself.

But if there's one thing I learned from Rodrick, it's to set people's expectations real low so you end up surprising them by practically doing nothing at all.

Actually, I'm kind of glad my plan to get put in the Easy group didn't work.

I saw a couple of the "Bink Says Boo" kids holding their books upside down, and I don't think they were joking.

Saturday
Well, the first week of school is finally over, so today I slept in.

Most kids wake up early on Saturday to watch cartoons or whatever, but not me. The only reason I get out of bed at all on weekends is because eventually, I can't stand the taste of my own breath anymore.

Unfortunately, Dad wakes up at 6:00 in the morning no matter WHAT day of the week it is, and he is not real considerate of the fact that I am trying to enjoy my Saturday like a normal person.

I didn't have anything to do today so I just headed up to Rowley's house.

Rowley is technically my best friend, but that is definitely subject to* change.

I've been avoiding Rowley since the first day of school, when he did something that really annoyed me.

* be subject to...
易受……的,
容易……

We were getting our stuff from our lockers at the end of the day, and Rowley came up to me and said—

I have told Rowley at least a billion times that now that we're in middle school, you're supposed to say "hang out*," not "play." But no matter how many noogies* I give him, he always forgets the next time.

* hang out
混
* noogie
敲脑门

I've been trying to be a lot more careful about my image ever since I got to middle school. But having Rowley around is definitely not helping.

I met Rowley a few years ago when he moved into my neighborhood.

His mom bought him this book called "How to Make Friends in New Places," and he came to my house trying all these dumb gimmicks.

I guess I kind of felt sorry for Rowley, and I decided to take him under my wing.

It's been great having him around, mostly because I get to use all the tricks Rodrick pulls on ME.

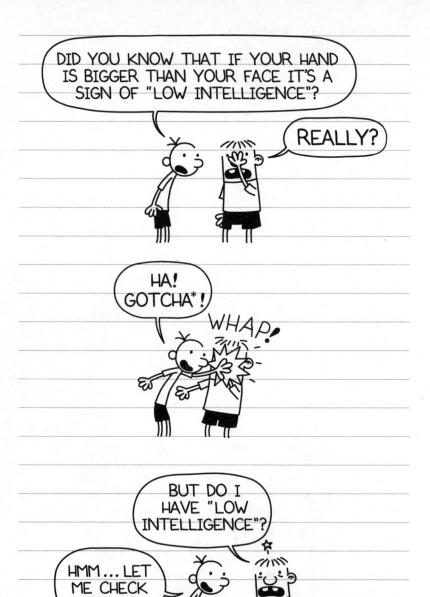

* gotcha
抓到你了
（get you
的缩写）

Monday

You know how I said I play all sorts of pranks on Rowley? Well, I have a little brother named Manny, and I could NEVER get away with pulling any of that stuff on him.

Mom and Dad protect Manny like he's a prince or something. And he never gets in trouble, even if he really deserves it.

Yesterday, Manny drew a self-portrait on my bedroom door in permanent marker. I thought Mom and Dad were really going to let him have it, but as usual, I was wrong.

But the thing that bugs me the most about Manny is the nickname he has for me. When he was a baby, he couldn't pronounce "brother," so he started calling me "Bubby." And he STILL calls me that now, even though I keep trying to get Mom and Dad to make him stop.

Luckily none of my friends have found out yet, but believe me, I have had some really close calls*.

* close call
幸免于难，
千钧一发

112

Mom makes me help Manny get ready for school in the morning. After I make Manny his breakfast, he carries his cereal bowl into the family room and sits on his plastic potty.

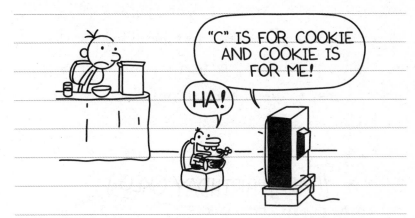

And when it's time for him to go to day care, he gets up and dumps whatever he didn't eat right in the toilet.

Mom is always getting on me about not finishing my breakfast. But if she had to scrape corn flakes out of the bottom of a plastic potty every morning, she wouldn't have much of an appetite either.

<u>Tuesday</u>

I don't know if I mentioned this before, but I am SUPER good at video games. I'll bet I could beat anyone in my grade head-to-head.

Unfortunately, Dad does not exactly appreciate my skills. He's always getting on me about going out and doing something "active."

So tonight after dinner when Dad started hassling me about going outside, I tried to explain how with video games, you can play sports like football and soccer, and you don't even get all hot and sweaty.

But as usual, Dad didn't see my logic.

Dad is a pretty smart guy in general but when it comes to common sense, sometimes I wonder about him.

I'm sure Dad would dismantle my game system if he could figure out how to do it. But luckily, the people who make these things make them parent-proof.

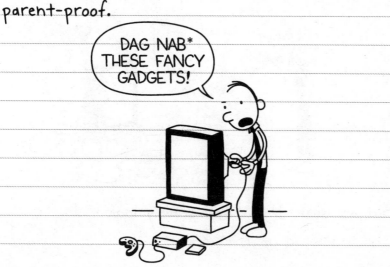

Every time Dad kicks me out of the house to do something sporty, I just go up to Rowley's and play my video games there.

Unfortunately, the only games I can play at Rowley's are car-racing games and stuff like that.

Because whenever I bring a game up to Rowley's house, his dad looks it up on some parents' Web site. And if my game has ANY kind of fighting or violence in it, he won't let us play.

HMMMM...

I'm getting a little sick of playing Formula One Racing with Rowley, because he's not a serious gamer like me. All that you have to do to beat Rowley is name your car something ridiculous at the beginning of the game.

And then when you pass Rowley's car, he just falls to pieces.

Anyway, after I got done mopping the floor with Rowley today, I headed home. I ran through the neighbor's sprinkler a couple times to make it look like I was all sweaty, and that seemed to do the trick for Dad.

But my trick kind of backfired, because as soon as Mom saw me, she made me go upstairs and take a shower.

Wednesday
I guess Dad must have been pretty happy with himself for making me go outside yesterday, because he did it again today.

It's getting really annoying to have to go up to Rowley's every time I want to play a video game. There's this weird kid named Fregley who lives halfway between my house and Rowley's, and Fregley is always hanging out in his front yard. So it's pretty hard to avoid him.

WANNA SEE MY "SECRET FRECKLE"?

UM...NO THANKS.

Fregley is in my Phys Ed class at school, and he has this whole made-up language. Like when he needs to go to the bathroom, he says—

Us kids have pretty much figured Fregley out by now, but I don't think the teachers have really caught on yet.

* gee whiz
唉呀，表示
感到意外，
吃惊的意思

Today, I probably would have gone up to Rowley's on my own anyway, because my brother Rodrick and his band were practicing down in the basement.

Rodrick's band is REALLY awful, and I can't stand being home when they're having rehearsals.

His band is called "Loaded Diaper," only it's spelled "Löded Diper" on Rodrick's van.

You might think he spelled it that way to make it look cooler, but I bet if you told Rodrick how "Loaded Diaper" is really spelled, it would be news to him.

Dad was against the idea of Rodrick starting a band, but Mom was all for it.

She's the one who bought Rodrick his first drum set.

I think Mom has this idea that we're all going to learn to play instruments and then become one of those family bands like you see on TV.

Dad really hates heavy metal, and that's the kind of music Rodrick and his band play. I don't think Mom really cares what Rodrick plays or listens to, because to her, all music is the same. In fact, earlier today, Rodrick was listening to one of his CDs in the family room, and Mom came in and started dancing.

That really bugged Rodrick, so he drove off to
the store and came back fifteen minutes later
with some headphones. And that pretty much
took care of the problem.

Thursday
Yesterday Rodrick got a new heavy metal CD,
and it had one of those "Parental Warning"
stickers on it.

I have never gotten to listen to one of those
Parental Warning CDs, because Mom and Dad never
let me buy them at the mall. So I realized the only
way I was gonna get a chance to listen to
Rodrick's CD was if I snuck it out of the house.

This morning, after Rodrick left, I called up Rowley
and told him to bring his CD player to school.

Then I went down to Rodrick's room and took
the CD off his rack.

You're not allowed to bring personal music players
to school, so we had to wait to use it until after
lunch when the teachers let us outside. As soon
as we got the chance, me and Rowley snuck
around the back of the school and loaded up
Rodrick's CD.

But Rowley forgot to put batteries in his CD
player, so it was pretty much worthless.

Then I came up with this great idea for a game.
The object was to put the headphones on your
head and then try to shake them off without
using your hands.

The winner was whoever could shake the headphones off in the shortest amount of time.

I had the record with seven and a half seconds, but I think I might have shook some of my fillings* loose with that one.

* filling
此处指牙齿
填充物

Right in the middle of our game, Mrs. Craig came around the corner and caught us red-handed. She took the music player away from me and started chewing us out.

But I think she had the wrong idea about what we were doing back there. She started telling us how rock and roll is "evil" and how it's going to ruin our brains.

I was going to tell her that there weren't even any batteries in the CD player, but I could tell she didn't want to be interrupted. So I just waited until she was done, and then I said, "Yes, ma'am."

But right when Mrs. Craig was about to let us go, Rowley started blubbering about how he doesn't want rock and roll to ruin his "brains."

Honestly, sometimes I don't know about that boy.

Friday

Well, now I've gone and done it.

Last night, after everyone was in bed, I snuck downstairs to listen to Rodrick's CD on the stereo in the family room.

I put Rodrick's new headphones on and cranked up the volume REALLY high. Then I hit "play."

First, let me just say I can definitely understand why they put that "Parental Warning" sticker on the CD.

But I only got to hear about thirty seconds of the first song before I got interrupted.

It turns out I didn't have the headphones plugged into the stereo. So the music was actually coming through the SPEAKERS, not the headphones.

Dad marched me up to my room and shut the door behind him, and then he said—

Whenever Dad says "friend" that way, you know you're in trouble. The first time Dad ever said "friend" like that to me, I didn't get that he was being sarcastic. So I kind of let my guard down.

I don't make that mistake anymore.

Tonight, Dad yelled at me for about ten minutes, and then I guess he decided he'd rather be in bed than standing in my room in his underwear. He told me I was grounded* from playing video games for two weeks, which is about what I expected. I guess I should be glad that's all he did.

The good thing about Dad is that when he gets mad, he cools off real quick, and then it's over.

* ground
禁止飞行员
或飞机飞
行，引申为
禁止小孩子
玩

Usually, if you mess up in front of Dad, he just throws whatever he's got in his hands at you.

GOOD TIME TO SCREW UP:

BAD TIME TO SCREW UP:

Mom has a TOTALLY different style when it comes to punishment. If you mess up and Mom catches you, the first thing she does is to take a few days to figure out what your punishment should be.

And while you're waiting, you do all these nice
things to try to get off easier.

But then after a few days, right when YOU
forget you're in trouble, that's when she lays it
on you.

<u>Monday</u>
This video game ban is a whole lot tougher than
I thought it would be. But at least I'm not the
only one in the family who's in trouble.

Rodrick's in some hot water with Mom right now,
too. Manny got ahold of one of Rodrick's heavy
metal magazines, and one of the pages had a
picture of a woman in a bikini lying across the
hood of a car. And then Manny brought it into
day care for show-and-tell.

Anyway, I don't think Mom was too happy about
getting that phone call.

I saw the magazine myself, and it honestly wasn't
anything to get worked up over. But Mom doesn't
allow that kind of stuff in the house.

Rodrick's punishment was that he had to answer
a bunch of questions Mom wrote out for him.

Did owning this magazine
make you a better person?

No.

Did it make you more
popular at school?

No.

How do you feel about having
owned this type of magazine
now?

I feel ashamed.

Do you have anything you
want to say to women for
having owned this offensive
magazine?

I'm sorry women.

<u>Wednesday</u>

I'm still grounded from playing video games, so Manny has been using my system. Mom went out and bought a whole bunch of educational video games, and watching Manny play them is like torture.

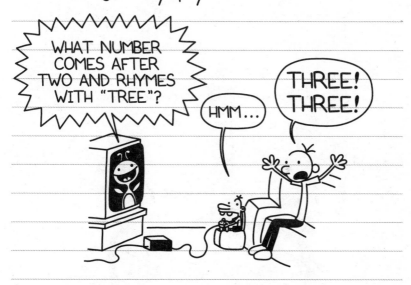

The good news is that I finally figured out how to get some of my games past Rowley's dad. I just put one of my discs in Manny's "Discovering the Alphabet" case, and that's all it takes.

<u>Thursday</u>

At school today, they announced that student government elections are coming up. To be honest with you, I've never had any interest in student government. But when I started thinking about it, I realized getting elected Treasurer could TOTALLY change my situation at school.

* nerd
书呆子（含贬义），一般指偏爱钻研书本知识，将大量闲暇用于读书，而不愿或不善于参加群体性活动的人

And even better...

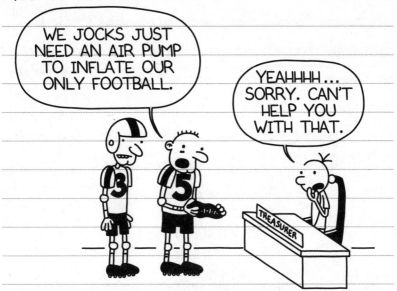

Nobody ever thinks about running for Treasurer, because all anyone ever cares about are the big-ticket positions like President and Vice President. So I figure if I sign up tomorrow, the Treasurer job is pretty much mine for the taking.

Friday
Today, I went and put my name on the list to run for Treasurer. Unfortunately, this kid named Marty Porter is running for Treasurer, too, and he's real brainy at math. So this might not be as easy as I thought.

I told Dad that I was running for student government, and he seemed pretty excited. It turns out he ran for student government when he was my age, and he actually won.

Dad dug through some old boxes in the basement and found one of his campaign posters.

INTEGRITY
HONESTY
KNOW-HOW

VOTE

Frank Heffley
FOR
SECRETARY

I thought the poster idea was pretty good, so I asked Dad to drive me to the store to get some supplies. I loaded up on poster board and markers, and I spent the rest of the night making all my campaign stuff. So let's just hope these posters work.

<u>Monday</u>

I brought my posters in to school today, and I have to say, they came out pretty good.

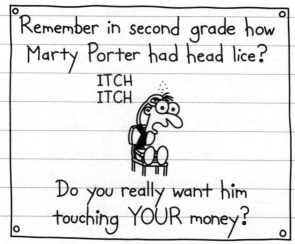

137

I started hanging my posters up as soon as I got in. But they were only up for about three minutes before Vice Principal Roy spotted them.

Mr. Roy said you weren't allowed to write "fabrications" about the other candidates. So I told Mr. Roy that the thing about the head lice was true, and how it practically closed down the whole school when it happened.

But he took down all my posters anyway. So today, Marty Porter was going around handing out lollipops to buy himself votes while my posters were sitting at the bottom of Mr. Roy's trash can. I guess this means my political career is officially over.

OCTOBER

<u>Monday</u>

Well, it's finally October, and there are only thirty days left until Halloween. Halloween is my FAVORITE holiday, even though Mom says I'm getting too old to go trick-or-treating anymore.

Halloween is Dad's favorite holiday, too, but for a different reason. On Halloween night, while all the other parents are handing out candy, Dad is hiding in the bushes with a big trash can full of water.

And if any teenagers pass by our driveway, he drenches them.

I'm not sure Dad really understands the concept of Halloween. But I'm not gonna be the one who spoils his fun.

Tonight was the opening night of the Crossland High School haunted house, and I got Mom to agree to take me and Rowley.

Rowley showed up at my house wearing his Halloween costume from last year. When I called him earlier I told him to just wear regular clothes, but of course he didn't listen.

I tried not to let it bother me too much, though. I've never been allowed to go to the Crossland haunted house before, and I wasn't going to let Rowley ruin it for me. Rodrick has told me all about it, and I've been looking forward to this for about three years.

Anyway, when we got to the entrance, I started having second thoughts about going in.

GOOD
EEEVENINGGG.

But Mom seemed like she was in a hurry to get this over with, and she moved us along. Once we were through the gate, it was one scare after another. There were vampires jumping out at you and people without heads and all sorts of crazy stuff.

But the worst part was this area called Chainsaw Alley. There was this big guy in a hockey mask and he had a REAL chainsaw. Rodrick told me the chainsaw has a rubber blade, but I wasn't taking any chances.

Right when it looked like the chainsaw guy was going to catch us, Mom stepped in and bailed us out.

Mom made the chainsaw guy show us where the exit was, and that was the end of our haunted house experience right there. I guess it was a little embarrassing when Mom did that, but I'm willing to let it go this one time.

Saturday
The Crossland haunted house really got me thinking. Those guys were charging five bucks a pop, and the line stretched halfway around the school.

I decided to make a haunted house of my own. Actually, I had to bring Rowley in on the deal, because Mom wouldn't let me convert our first floor into a full-out haunted mansion.

I knew Rowley's dad wouldn't be crazy about the idea, either, so we decided to build the haunted house in his basement and just not mention it to his parents.

Me and Rowley spent most of the day coming up with an awesome plan for our haunted house.

Here was our final plan:

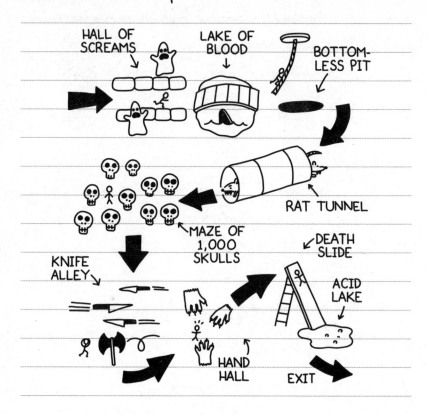

I don't mean to brag or anything, but what we came up with was WAY better than the Crossland High School haunted house.

We realized we were gonna need to get the word out that we were doing this thing, so we got some paper and made up a bunch of flyers.

I'll admit maybe we stretched the truth a little in our advertisement, but we had to make sure people actually showed up.

HAUNTED
H💀USE
(OUCH.)
WITH **LIVE** SHARKS!

32 SURREY STREET
ADMISSION : 50¢
3:00 p.m.

By the time we finished putting the flyers up around the neighborhood and got back to Rowley's basement, it was already 2:30, and we hadn't even started putting the actual haunted house together yet.

So we had to cut some corners from our original plan.

When 3:00 rolled around, we looked outside to
see if anyone had showed up. And sure enough,
there were about twenty neighborhood kids waiting
in line outside Rowley's basement.

Now, I know our flyers said admission was fifty
cents, but I could see that we had a chance to
make a killing* here.

So I told the kids that admission was two bucks,
and the fifty-cent thing was just a typo.

The first kid to cough up his two bucks was
Shane Snella. He paid his money and we let him
inside, and me and Rowley took our positions in
the Hall of Screams.

The Hall of Screams was basically a bed with me
and Rowley on either side of it.

I guess maybe we made the Hall of Screams a
little too scary, because halfway through, Shane
curled up in a ball underneath the bed. We tried
to get him to crawl out from under there, but
he wouldn't budge.

I started thinking about all the money we were
losing with this kid clogging up the Hall of Screams,
and I knew we had to get him out of there, quick.

Eventually, Rowley's dad came downstairs. At
first I was happy to see him, because I thought
he could help us drag Shane out from under the
bed and get our haunted house cranking* again.

* crank
开始

147

But Rowley's dad wasn't really in a helpful mood.

POKE
POKE

Rowley's dad wanted to know what we were
doing, and why Shane Snella was curled up under
the bed.

We told him that the basement was a haunted
house, and that Shane Snella actually PAID
for us to do this to him. But Rowley's dad didn't
believe us.

I admit that if you looked around, it didn't
really look like a haunted house. All we had time
to put together was the Hall of Screams and the
Lake of Blood, which was just Rowley's old baby
pool with half a bottle of ketchup in it.

I tried to show Rowley's dad our original plan to prove that we really were running a legitimate operation, but he still didn't seem convinced.

And to make a long story short, that was the end of our haunted house.

The good news is, since Rowley's dad didn't believe us, he didn't make us refund Shane's money. So at least we cleared two bucks today.

<u>Sunday</u>
Rowley ended up getting grounded for that whole haunted house mess yesterday. He's not allowed to watch TV for a week, AND he's not allowed to have me over at his house during that time.

That last part really isn't fair, because that's punishing me, and I didn't even do anything wrong. And now where am I supposed to play my video games?

Anyway, I felt kind of bad for Rowley. So tonight, I tried to make it up to him. I turned on one of Rowley's favorite TV shows, and I did a play-by-play over the phone so he could kind of experience it that way.

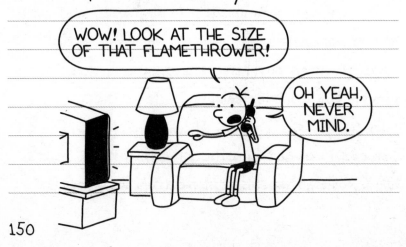

WOW! LOOK AT THE SIZE OF THAT FLAMETHROWER!

OH YEAH, NEVER MIND.

I did my best to keep up with what was going on on the screen, but to be honest with you, I'm not sure if Rowley was getting the full effect.

Tuesday
Well, Rowley's grounding is finally over, and just in time for Halloween, too. I went up to his house to check out his costume, and I have to admit, I'm a little jealous.

Rowley's Mom got him this knight costume that's WAY cooler than his costume from last year.

His knight outfit came with a helmet and a shield
and a real sword and EVERYTHING.

I've never had a store-bought costume before. I
still haven't figured out what I'm gonna go as
tomorrow night, so I'll probably just throw
something together* at the last minute. I figure
maybe I'll bring back the Toilet Paper Mummy again.

* throw
together
东拼西凑

But I think it's supposed to rain tomorrow
night, so that might not be the smartest choice.

In the past few years, the grown-ups in my neighborhood have been getting cranky about my lame costumes, and I'm starting to think it's actually having an effect on the amount of candy I'm bringing in.

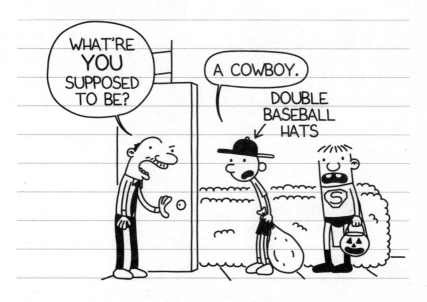

But I don't really have time to put together a good costume, because I'm in charge of planning out the best route for me and Rowley to take tomorrow night.

This year I've come up with a plan that'll get us at least twice the candy we scored last year.

Halloween

About an hour before we were supposed to start trick-or-treating, I still didn't have a costume. At that point I was seriously thinking about going as a cowboy for the second year in a row.

But then Mom knocked at my door and handed me a pirate costume, with an eye patch and a hook and everything.

Rowley showed up around 6:30 wearing his knight costume, but it didn't look ANYTHING like it looked yesterday.

Rowley's mom made all these safety improvements to it, and you couldn't even tell what he was supposed to be anymore.

She cut out a big hole in the front of the helmet so he could see better, and covered him up in all this reflective tape. She made him wear his winter coat underneath everything, and she replaced his sword with a glow stick.

I grabbed my pillowcase, and me and Rowley started to head out. But Mom stopped us before we could get out the door.

I WANT YOU TO TAKE MANNY WITH YOU!

Man, I should have known there was a catch when Mom gave me that costume.

I told Mom there was no WAY we were taking Manny with us, because we were going to hit 152 houses in three hours. And plus, we were going to be on Snake Road, which is way too dangerous for a little kid like Manny.

I should never have mentioned that last part, because the next thing I knew, Mom was telling Dad he had to go along with us to make sure we didn't step foot outside our neighborhood. Dad tried to squirm out of* it, but once Mom makes up her mind, there's no way you can change it.

* squirm
out of...
摆脱……

Before we even got out of our own driveway, we ran into our neighbor Mr. Mitchell and his kid Jeremy. So of course THEY tagged along with us.

Manny and Jeremy wouldn't trick-or-treat at any houses with spooky decorations on them, so that ruled out pretty much every house on our block.

Dad and Mr. Mitchell started talking about football or something, and every time one of them wanted to make a point, they'd stop walking.

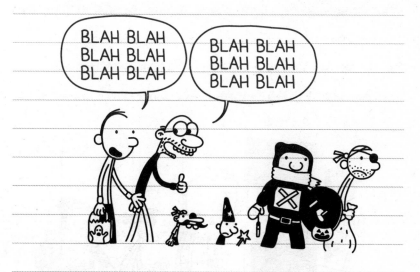

So we were hitting only about one house every twenty minutes.

After a couple of hours, Dad and Mr. Mitchell took the little kids home.

I was glad, because that meant me and Rowley could take off. My pillowcase was almost empty, so I wanted to make up as much time as possible.

A little while later, Rowley told me he needed a "potty break." I made him hold off for another forty-five minutes. But by the time we got to my gramma's house, it was pretty clear that if I didn't let Rowley use the bathroom, it was gonna get messy.

So I told Rowley if he wasn't back outside in one minute, I was gonna start helping myself to his candy.

After that, we headed back out on the road. But it was already 10:30, and I guess that's when most grown-ups decide Halloween is over.

You can kind of tell because that's when they start coming to the door in their pajamas and giving you the evil eye.

We decided to head home. We made up a lot of time after Dad and Manny left, so I was pretty satisfied with how much candy we took in.

When we were halfway home, this pickup truck came roaring down the street with a bunch of high school kids in it.

The kid in the back was holding a fire extinguisher, and when the truck passed by us, he opened fire.

I have to give Rowley credit, because he blocked about 95% of the water with his shield. And if he hadn't done that, all our candy would have gotten soaked.

When the truck drove away, I yelled out something that I regretted about two seconds later.

The driver slammed on the brakes and he turned his truck around. Me and Rowley started running, but those guys were right on our heels.

The only place I could think of that was safe was Gramma's house, so we cut through a couple backyards to get there. Gramma was in bed already, but I knew she keeps a key under the mat on her front porch.

Once we got inside, I looked out the window to see if those guys had followed us, and sure enough, they did. I tried to trick them into leaving, but they wouldn't budge.

WELL, I GUESS NOW THAT WE'RE SAFE IN OUR OWN HOUSE, YOU CAN'T GET US!

After a while, we realized the teenagers were going to wait us out, so we decided we were just gonna have to spend the night at Gramma's. That's when we started getting cocky, making monkey noises at the teenagers and whatnot.

Well, at least I was making monkey noises. Rowley was kind of making owl noises, but I guess it was the same general idea.

* crash
找到临时寄
宿或避难的
地方

I called Mom to tell her we were going to crash* at Gramma's for the night. But Mom sounded really mad on the phone.

She said it was a school night, and that we had to get home right that instant. So that meant we were gonna have to make a run for it.

I looked out the window, and this time, I didn't see the truck. But I knew those guys were hiding somewhere and were just trying to draw us out.

So we snuck out the back door, hopped over Gramma's fence, and ran all the way to Snake Road. I figured our chances were better there because there aren't any streetlights.

Snake Road is scary enough on its own without having a truckload of teenagers hunting you down. Every time we saw a car coming, we dove into the bushes. It must've taken us a half hour to go 100 yards.

But believe it or not, we made it all the way home without getting caught. Neither one of us let our guard down until we got to my driveway.

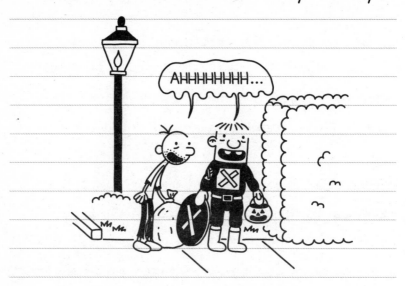

But right then, there was this awful scream, and we saw a big wave of water coming toward us.

Man, I forgot ALL about Dad, and we totally paid the price for it.

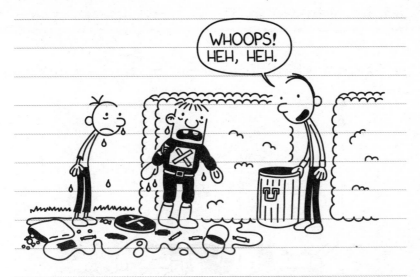

When me and Rowley got inside, we laid out all our candy on the kitchen table.

The only things we could salvage were a couple of mints that were wrapped in cellophane, and the toothbrushes Dr. Garrison gave us.

I think next Halloween I'll just stay home and mooch some Butterfingers from the bowl Mom keeps on top of the refrigerator.

<u>Thursday</u>

On the bus ride into school today, we passed by Gramma's house. It got rolled with toilet paper last night, which I guess was no big surprise.

I do feel a little bad, because it looked like it was gonna take a long time to clean up. But on the bright side, Gramma is retired, so she probably didn't have anything planned for today anyway.

<u>Wednesday</u>

In third period, Mr. Underwood, our Phys Ed teacher, announced that the boys will be doing a wrestling unit for the next six weeks.

If there's one thing most boys in my school are into, it's professional wrestling. So Mr. Underwood might as well have set off a bomb.

Lunch comes right after Phys Ed, and the cafeteria was a complete madhouse.

I don't know what the school is thinking having a wrestling unit.

But I decided if I don't want to get twisted into a pretzel* for the next month and a half, I'd better do my homework on this wrestling business.

* pretzel 椒盐卷饼，2002年美国总统布什便是吃这种饼干时噎塞喉咙而晕倒

So I rented a couple of video games to learn
some moves. And you know what? After a while,
I was really starting to get the hang of it.

In fact, the other kids in my class had better
look out, because if I keep this up, I could be a
real threat.

Then again, I better make sure I don't do TOO good. This kid named Preston Mudd got named Athlete of the Month for being the best player in the basketball unit, so they put his picture up in the hallway.

It took people about five seconds to realize how "P. Mudd" sounded when you said it out loud, and after that, it was all over for Preston.

Thursday

Well, I found out today that the kind of wrestling Mr. Underwood is teaching is COMPLETELY different from the kind they do on TV.

First of all, we have to wear these things called "singlets," which look like those bathing suits they used to wear in the 1800s.

And second of all, there are no pile drivers or hitting people over the heads with chairs or anything like that.

There's not even a ring with ropes around it. It's just basically a sweaty mat that smells like it's never been washed before.

Mr. Underwood started asking for volunteers so he could demonstrate some wrestling holds, but there was no way I was going to raise my hand.

Me and Rowley tried to hide out in the back of the gym near the curtain, but that's where the girls were doing their gymnastics unit.

We got out of there in a hurry, and we went back to where the rest of the guys were.

Mr. Underwood singled me out, probably because I'm the lightest kid in the class, and he could toss me around without straining himself. He showed everybody how to do all these things called a "half nelson" and a "reversal" and a "takedown" and stuff like that.

When he was doing this one move called the "fire-man's carry," I felt a breeze down below, and I could tell my singlet wasn't doing a good job keeping me covered up.

That's when I thanked my lucky stars the girls were on the other side of the gym.

Mr. Underwood divided us up into weight groups. I was pretty happy about that at first, because it meant I wasn't going to have to wrestle kids like Benny Wells, who can bench-press 250 pounds.

But then I found out who I DID have to wrestle, and I would have traded for Benny Wells in a heartbeat.

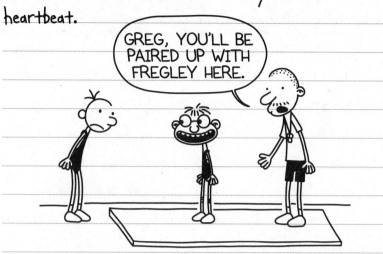

GREG, YOU'LL BE PAIRED UP WITH FREGLEY HERE.

Fregley was the only kid light enough to be in my weight class. And apparently Fregley was paying attention when Mr. Underwood was giving instructions, because he pinned me every which way you could imagine. I spent my seventh period getting WAY more familiar with Fregley than I ever wanted to be.

TWEET!

<u>Tuesday</u>

This wrestling unit has totally turned our school upside down. Now kids are wrestling in the hallways, in the classrooms, you name it. But the fifteen minutes after lunch where they let us outside is the worst.

You can't walk five feet without tripping over a couple of kids going at it. I just try to keep my distance. And mark my words, one of these fools is going to roll right onto the Cheese and start the Cheese Touch all over again.

My other big problem is that I have to wrestle Fregley every single day.- But this morning I realized something. If I can move out of Fregley's weight class, I won't have to wrestle him anymore.

So today, I stuffed my clothes with a bunch of socks and shirts to get myself into the next weight class.

But I was still too light to move up.

I realized I was gonna have to gain weight for real. At first I thought I should just start loading up on junk food, but then I had a much better idea.

I decided to gain my weight in MUSCLE, not fat.

I've never been all that interested in getting in shape before, but this wrestling unit has made me rethink things.

I figure if I bulk up now, it could actually come in handy down the road.

The football unit is coming in the spring, and they split the teams up into shirts and skins. And I ALWAYS get put on skins.

I think they do that to make all the out-of-shape kids feel ashamed of themselves.

If I can pack on some muscle now, it'll be a whole different story next April.

Tonight, after dinner, I got Mom and Dad together and told them my plan. I told them I was going to need some serious exercise equipment, and some weight-gain powder, too.

I showed them some muscle magazines I got at the store so they could see how ripped I was going to be.

Mom didn't really say anything at first, but Dad was pretty enthusiastic. I think he was just glad I had a change of heart from how I used to be when I was a kid—

But Mom said if I wanted a weight set, I was going to have to prove that I could stick with an exercise regimen. She said I could do that by doing sit-ups and jumping jacks for two weeks.

I had to explain that the only way to get totally bulked up is to get the kind of high-tech machines they have at the gym, but Mom didn't want to hear it.

Then Dad said if I wanted a bench press, I should keep my fingers crossed for Christmas.

But Christmas is a month and a half away. And if I get pinned by Fregley one more time, I'm gonna have a nervous breakdown.

So it looks like Mom and Dad aren't going to be any help. And that means I'm going to have to take matters into my own hands, as usual.

Saturday
I couldn't wait to start my weight-training program today. Even though Mom wouldn't let me get the equipment I needed, I wasn't going to let that hold me back.

So I went into the fridge and emptied out the milk and orange juice and filled the jugs with sand. Then I taped them to a broomstick, and I had myself a pretty decent barbell.

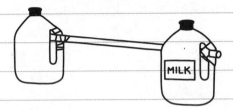

After that, I made a bench press out of an ironing board and some boxes. Once I had that all set, I was ready to do some serious lifting.

I needed a spotting partner, so I called Rowley. And when he showed up at my door wearing some ridiculous getup, I knew I made a mistake inviting him.

I made Rowley use the bench press first, mostly because I wanted to see if the broomstick was going to hold up.

He did about five reps, and he was ready to quit, but I wouldn't let him. That's what a good training partner is for, to push you beyond your limits.

FIFTEEN MORE! COME ON!

I knew Rowley wasn't going to be as serious about weight lifting as I was, so I decided to try out an experiment to test his dedication.

In the middle of Rowley's set, I went and got this phony nose and mustache Rodrick has in his junk drawer.

And right when Rowley had the barbell in the "down" position, I leaned over and looked at him.

Sure enough, Rowley TOTALLY lost his concentration. He couldn't even get the barbell off his chest. I thought about helping him out, but then I realized that if Rowley didn't get serious about working out, he was never going to get to my level.

I eventually had to rescue him, because he started biting the milk jug to let the sand leak out.

After Rowley got off the bench press, it was time for my set. But Rowley said he didn't feel like working out anymore, and he went home.

You know, I figured he'd pull something like that. But I guess you can't expect everyone to have the same kind of dedication as you.

Wednesday
Today in Geography we had a quiz, and I have to say, I've been looking forward to this one for a long time.

The quiz was on state capitals, and I sit in the back of the room, right next to this giant map of the United States. All the capitals are written in big red print, so I knew I had this one in the bag.

But right before the test got started, Patty
Farrell piped up from the front of the room.

Patty told Mr. Ira that he should cover up the
United States map before we got started.

So thanks to Patty, I ended up flunking the
quiz. And I will definitely be looking for a way
to pay her back for that one.

<u>Thursday</u>
Tonight Mom came up to my room, and she had a
flyer in her hand. As soon as I saw it, I knew
EXACTLY what it was.

It was an announcement that the school is having
tryouts for a winter play. Man, I should have
thrown that thing out when I saw it on the
kitchen table.

I BEGGED her not to make me sign up. Those
school plays are always musicals, and the last
thing I need is to have to sing a solo in front
of the whole school.

But all my begging seemed to do was make Mom
more sure I should do it.

Mom said the only way I was going to be "well-rounded" was by trying different things.

Dad came in my room to see what was going on. I told Dad that Mom was making me sign up for the school play, and that if I had to start going to play practices, it would totally mess up my weight-lifting schedule.

I knew that would make Dad take my side. Dad and Mom argued for a few minutes, but Dad was no match for Mom.

So that means tomorrow I've got to audition for the school play.

Friday
The play they're doing this year is "The Wizard of Oz." A lot of kids came wearing costumes for the parts they were trying out for.

I've never even seen the movie, so for me, it was like walking into a freak show.

Mrs. Norton, the music director, made everyone sing "My Country 'Tis of Thee" so she could hear our singing voices. I did my singing tryouts with a bunch of other boys whose moms made them come, too. I tried to sing as quietly as possible, but of course I got singled out, anyway.

187

I have no idea what a "soprano" is, but from the way some of the girls were giggling, I knew it wasn't a good thing.

Tryouts went on forever. The grand finale came with auditions for Dorothy, who I guess is the lead character in the play.

And who should try out first but Patty Farrell.

I thought about trying out for the part of the Witch, because I heard that in the play, the Witch does all sorts of mean things to Dorothy.

But then somebody told me there's a Good Witch and a Bad Witch, and with my luck, I'd end up getting picked to be the good one.

<u>Monday</u>

I was hoping Mrs. Norton would just cut me from the play, but today she said that everyone who tried out is going to get a part. So lucky me.

Mrs. Norton showed "The Wizard of Oz" movie so everyone would know the story. I was trying to figure out what part I should play, but pretty much every character has to sing or dance at one point or another. But about halfway through the movie, I figured out what part I wanted to sign up for. I'm going to sign up to be a Tree, because 1) they don't have to sing and 2) they get to bean* Dorothy with apples.

* bean
用东西砸某
人头部

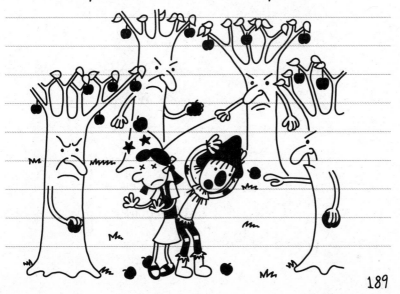

189

Getting to peg Patty Farrell with apples in front of a live audience would be my dream come true. I may actually have to thank Mom for making me do this play once it's all over.

After the movie ended, I signed up to be a Tree. Unfortunately, a bunch of other guys had the same idea as me, so I guess there are a lot of guys who have a bone to pick with* Patty Farrell.

* have a
bone to
pick with...
与……有过
节

Wednesday

Well, like Mom always says, be careful what you wish for. I got picked to be a Tree, but I don't know if that's such a good thing. The Tree costumes don't actually have arm holes, so I guess that rules out any apple-throwing.

I should probably feel lucky that I got a speaking part at all. They had too many kids trying out, and not enough roles, so they had to start making up characters.

Rodney James tried out to be the Tin Man, but he got stuck with being the Shrub.

Friday

Remember how I said I was lucky to get a speaking part? Well, today I found out I only have one line in the whole play. I say it when Dorothy picks an apple off my branch.

That means I have to go to a two-hour practice every day just so I can say one stupid word.

I'm starting to think Rodney James got a better deal as the Shrub. He found a way to sneak a video game into his costume, and I'll bet that really makes the time go by.

So now I'm trying to think of ways to get Mrs. Norton to kick me out of the play. But when you only have one word to say, it's really hard to mess up your lines.

DECEMBER

<u>Thursday</u>

The play is only a couple of days away, and I have no idea how we're going to pull this thing off.

First of all, nobody has bothered to learn their lines, and that's all Mrs. Norton's fault.

During rehearsal, Mrs. Norton whispers everyone's lines to them from the side of the stage.

I wonder how it's going to go next Tuesday when Mrs. Norton is sitting at her piano thirty feet away.

Another thing that's screwing everything up is that Mrs. Norton keeps adding new scenes and new characters.

Yesterday, she brought in this first-grader to play Dorothy's dog, Toto. But today, the kid's mom came in and said she wanted her child to walk around on two legs, because crawling around on all fours would be too "degrading."

So now we've got a dog that's gonna be walking around on his hind legs for the whole show.

But the worst change is that Mrs. Norton actually wrote a song that us TREES have to sing. She said everyone "deserves" a chance to sing in the play.

So today we spent an hour learning the worst
song that's ever been written.

Thank God Rodrick won't be in the audience to
see me humiliate myself. Mrs. Norton said the
play is going to be a "semiformal occasion," and I
know there's no way Rodrick is going to wear a
tie for a middle school play.

But today wasn't all bad. Toward the end of
practice, Archie Kelly tripped over Rodney James
and chipped his tooth because he couldn't stick
his arms out to break his fall.

GAAH!

So the good news is, they're letting us Trees carve out arm holes for the performance.

Tuesday
Tonight was the big school production of "The Wizard of Oz." The first sign that things were not going to go well happened before the play even started.

I was peeking through the curtain to check out how many people showed up to see the play, and guess who was standing right up front? My brother Rodrick, wearing a clip-on tie.

He must have found out I was singing, and he couldn't resist the chance to see me embarrass myself.

The play was supposed to start at 8:00, but it got delayed because Rodney James had stage fright.

You'd figure that someone whose job it was to sit on the stage and do nothing could just suck it up for one performance. But Rodney wouldn't budge, and eventually, his mom had to carry him off.

The play finally got started around 8:30. Nobody could remember their lines, just like I predicted, but Mrs. Norton kept things moving along with her piano.

The kid who played Toto brought a stool and a
pile of comic books onto the stage, and that
totally ruined the whole "dog" effect.

When it was time for the forest scene, me and
the other Trees hopped into our positions. The
curtains rose, and when they did, I heard
Manny's voice.

198

Great. I have been able to keep that nickname quiet for five years, and now all of the sudden the whole town knew it. I could feel about 300 pairs of eyeballs pointed my way.

So I did some quick ad-libbing* and I was able to deflect the embarrassment over to Archie Kelly.

* ad-lib
即兴表演

But the major embarrassment was still on the way. When I heard Mrs. Norton playing the first few bars of "We Three Trees," I felt my stomach jump.

I looked out at the audience, and I noticed Rodrick was holding a video camera.

I knew that if I sang the song and Rodrick recorded it, he would keep the tape forever and use it to humiliate me for the rest of my life.

I didn't know what to do, so when the time came to start singing, I just kept my mouth shut.

For a few seconds there, things went OK. I figured that if I didn't technically sing the song, then Rodrick wouldn't have anything to hold over my head*. But after a few seconds, the other Trees noticed I wasn't singing.

* hold over
one's head
反复提醒某
人

200

I guess they must've thought I knew something that they didn't, so they stopped singing, too.

Now the three of us were just standing there, not saying a word. Mrs. Norton must have thought we forgot the words to the song, because she came over to the side of the stage and whispered the rest of the lyrics to us.

The song is only about three minutes long, but to me it felt like an hour and a half. I was just praying the curtains would go down so we could hop off the stage.

That's when I noticed Patty Farrell standing in the wings. And if looks could kill, us Trees would be dead. She probably thought we were ruining her chances of making it to Broadway or something.

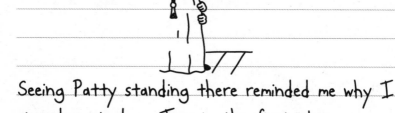

Seeing Patty standing there reminded me why I signed up to be a Tree in the first place.

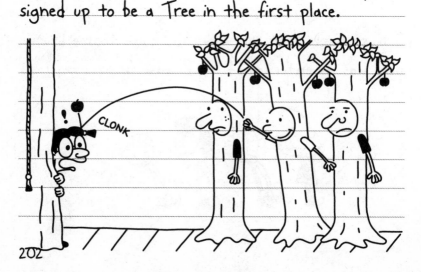

Pretty soon, the rest of the Trees started throwing apples, too. I think Toto even got in on the act.

Somebody knocked the glasses off of Patty's head, and one of the lenses broke. Mrs. Norton had to shut down the play after that, because Patty can't see two feet in front of her without her glasses.

After the play was over, my family went home together. Mom had brought a bouquet of flowers, and I guess they were supposed to be for me. But she ended up tossing them in the trash can on the way out the door.

I just hope that everyone who came to see the play was as entertained as I was.

望子快乐

朱子庆

　　在一个人的一生中，"与有荣焉"的机会或有，但肯定不多。因为儿子译了一部畅销书，而老爸被邀涂鸦几句，像这样的与荣，我想，即使放眼天下，也没有几人领得吧。

　　儿子接活儿翻译《小屁孩日记》时，还在读着大三。这是安安第一次领译书稿，多少有点紧张和兴奋吧，起初他每译几段，便飞鸽传书，不一会儿人也跟过来，在我面前"项庄舞剑"地问："有意思么？有意思么？"怎么当时我就没有作乐不可支状呢？于今想来，我竟很有些后悔。对于一个喂饱段子与小品的中国人，若说还有什么洋幽默能令我们"绝倒"，难！不过，当安安译成杀青之时，图文并茂，我得以从头到尾再读一遍，我得说，这部书岂止有意思呢，读了它使我有一种冲动，假如时间可以倒流，我很想尝试重新做一回父亲！我不免窃想，安安在译它的时候，不知会怎样腹诽我这个老爸呢！

　　我宁愿儿子是书里那个小屁孩！

　　你可能会说，你别是在做秀吧，小屁孩格雷将来能出息成个什么样子，实在还很难说……这个质疑，典型地出诸一个中国人之口，出之于为父母的中国人之口。望子成龙，一定要孩子出息成个什么样子，虽说初衷也是为了孩子，但最终却是苦了孩子。"生年不满百，常怀千岁忧。"现在，由于这深重的忧患，我们已经把成功学启示的模式都做到胎教了！而望子快乐，有谁想过？从小就快乐，快乐一生？惭愧，我也是看了《小屁孩日记》才想到这点，然而儿子已不再年少！我觉得很有些对不住儿子！

　　我从来没有对安安的"少年老成"感到过有什么不妥，毕竟少年老成使人放心。而今读其译作而被触动，此心才为之不安起来。我在想，比起美国的小屁孩格雷和他的同学们，我们中国的小屁孩们是不是活得不很小屁孩？是不是普遍地过于负重、乏乐和少年老成？而当他们将来长大，娶妻（嫁夫）生子（女），为人父母，会不会还要循此逻辑再造下一代？想想安安少年时，起早贪黑地读书、写作业，小四眼，十足一个书呆子，类似格雷那样的调皮、贪玩、小有恶搞、缰绳牢笼不住地敢于尝试和行动主义……太缺少了。印象中，安安最突出的一次，也就是读小学三年级时，做了一回带头大哥，拔了校园里所有单车的气门芯并四处派发，仅此而已吧（此处，请在家长指导下阅读）。

　　说点别的吧。中国作家写的儿童文学作品，很少能引发成年读者的阅读兴趣。安徒生童话之所以风靡天下，在于它征服了成年读者。在我看来，《小屁孩日记》也属于成人少年兼宜的读物，可以父子同修！谁没有年少轻狂？谁没有豆蔻年华？只不过呢，对于为父母者，阅读它，会使你由会心一笑而再笑，继以感慨系之，进而不免有所自省，对照和检讨一下自己和孩子的关系，以及在某些类似事情的处理上，自己是否欠妥？等等。它虽系成人所作，书中对孩子心性的把握，却准确传神；虽非心理学著作，对了解孩子的心理和行为，也不无参悟和启示。品学兼优和顽劣不学的孩子毕竟是少数，小屁孩格雷是"中间人物"的一个玲珑典型，着实招人怜爱——在格雷身上，有着我们彼此都难免有的各样小心思、小算计、小毛病，就好像阿Q，读来透着与我们有那么一种割不断的血缘关系，这，也许就是此书在美国乃至全球都特别畅销的原因吧！

　　最后我想申明的是，第一读者身份在我是弥足珍惜的，因为，宝贝儿子出生时，第一眼看见他的是医生，老爸都摊不上第一读者呢！

我眼中的 😝 ……

好书，爱不释手！

★ 王汐子（女，19 岁，2009 年留学美国，攻读大学传媒专业）《小屁孩日记》在美国掀起的阅读风潮可不是盖的，在我留学美国的这一年中，不止一次目睹这套书对太平洋彼岸人民的巨大影响。高速公路上巨大的广告宣传牌就不用说了，我甚至在学校书店买课本时看到了这套书被大大咧咧地摆上书架，"小屁孩"的搞笑日记就这样理直气壮地充当起了美国大学生的课本教材！为什么这套书如此受欢迎？为什么一个普普通通的小男孩能让这么多成年人捧腹大笑？也许可以套用一个万能句式"每个人心中都有一个 XXX"。每个人心中都有一个小屁孩，每个人小时候也有过这样的时光，每天都有点鸡毛蒜皮的小烦恼，像作业这么多怎么办啦，要考试了书都没有看怎么办啦……但是大部分时候还是因为调皮捣乱被妈妈教训……就这样迷迷糊糊地走过了"小屁孩"时光，等长大后和朋友们讨论后才恍然大悟，随即不禁感慨，原来那时候我们都一样呀……是呀，全世界的小屁孩都一样！

★ 读者 书山有径（发表于 2010 - 01 - 31）这是一本真正写给孩子的书。作为圣诞礼物买给女儿，由于作业多，平时只能睡前读几页。放假了，女儿天天捧着这本书，一天到晚为书的人和事笑个不停；天天给我讲鬼屋的故事，用神秘而恐怖的语气。并且，天天问我，生活中她的朋友哪些应该被叫做"小屁孩"，怎么个"屁"法。

★ 读者 zhizhimother（发表于 2009 – 06 – 12）在杂志上看到这书的介绍，一时冲动在当当上下了单，没想到，一买回来一家人抢着看，笑得前仰后合。我跟女儿一人抢到一本，老公很不满意，他嘟囔着下一本出的时候他要第一个看。看多了面孔雷同的好孩子的书，看到这本，真是深有感触，我们的孩子其实都是这样长大的～～

轻松阅读 捧腹大笑

★ 这是著名的畅销书作家小巫的儿子 Sam 口述的英语和中文读后感：*I like* Diary of a Wimpy Kid *because Greg is an average child just like us. His words are really funny and the illustrations are hilarious. His stories are eventful and most of them involve silliness.* 我喜欢《小屁孩日记》，因为 Greg 是跟我们一样的普通孩子。他的故事很好玩儿，令我捧腹大笑，他做的事情很搞笑，有点儿傻呼呼的。书里的插图也很幽默。

★ 读者 bnulizi（发表于 2009 – 06 – 08）同学在开心网里转帖推荐这套书，于是我便傻傻地买了一套。看后发现还是挺赞的，笑料很多啊。而且最精彩的地方往往都是通过一段文字后的那幅图来表达的，我笑到肚子痛……

★ 读者 dearm 暖 baby（发表于 2009 – 07 – 29）我 12 岁了，过生日时妈妈给我买了这样两本书，真的很有趣！一半是中文，一半是英文，彻底打破了"英文看不懂看下面中文"的局限！而且这本书彻底地给我来了次大放松，"重点中学"的压力也一扫而光！总之，两个字：超赞！

★ 读者 mei298（发表于 2010 – 01 – 23）儿子超喜欢，边看边

大笑。买了1~4册，没几天就看完了，特别喜欢那一段"弗雷格跟我在同一个班上体育课，他的语言自成一家，比如说他要去厕所的时候，他就说——果汁！果汁！！！我们已经大致清楚弗雷格那套了，不过我看老师们大概还没弄懂。老师说——好吧，小伙子……你可真难伺候！还端来了一杯汽水。"为了这段话，儿子笑了一整天，到睡觉的时候想想还笑。

孩子爱上写日记了！

★ 读者 *pinganfurong*（发表于2009 – 11 – 10）一直想让九岁的儿子记记日记，但始终不喜欢给他"布置任务"。生活啦、工作啦、学习啦、休闲啦、娱乐啦等等等等，都是自己的事，自己喜欢，才能做好。写文章、记日记，也是如此。给老师写，为爹妈记，是件很烦人的事。命题作文、任务日记，只会让孩子讨厌写作文，讨厌记日记。讨厌的事能干好？笑话！怎么办呢？怎样才能让儿子自觉自愿地喜欢上记日记呢？于是，给儿子买了《小屁孩日记》。果不其然，儿子读完后，便拉着我去给他买回一个又大又厚的日记本，兴趣盎然地记起日记来。

★ 读者 *ddian*2003（发表于2009 – 12 – 22）正是于丹的那几句话吸引我买下了这套书。自己倒没看，但女儿却用了三天学校的课余时间就看完了，随后她大受启发，连着几天都写了日记。现在这书暂时搁在书柜里，已和女儿约定，等她学了英文后再来看一遍，当然要看书里的英文了。所以这书还是买得物有所值的。毕竟女儿喜欢！！

做个"不听话的好孩子"

★ 读者 水真爽（发表于2010 – 03 – 27）这套书是买给我上小学二年级的儿子的。有时候他因为到该读书的时间而被要求从网游下来很恼火。尽管带着气，甚至眼泪，可是读起这本书来，总是能被书中小屁孩的种种淘气出格行为和想法弄得哈哈大笑。书中的卡通漫画也非常不错。这种文字漫画形式的日记非常具有趣味性，老少咸宜。对低年级孩子或爱画漫画的孩子尤其有启发作用。更重要的是提醒家长们好好留意观察这些"不怎么听话"的小屁孩们的内心世界，他们的健康成长需要成人的呵护引导，但千万不要把他们都变成只会"听大人话"的好孩子。

★ 读者 寂寞朱丽叶（发表于 2009 - 06 - 10）最近我身边的朋友都在看这本书，出于好奇我也买了一套，美国"囧男孩"格雷满脑子的鬼主意，虽然不是人们心目中好孩子的形象，但很真实，我很喜欢他，还有点羡慕他，我怎么没有他有趣呢。

对照《小屁孩日记》分享育儿体验

★ 读者 gjrzj2002@＊＊＊.＊＊＊（发表于 2010 - 05 - 21）看完四册书，我想着自己虽然不可能有三个孩子，但一个孩子的成长经历至今仍记忆犹新。儿子还是幼儿的时候，比较像曼尼，在爸妈眼中少有缺点，真是让人越看越爱，想要什么就基本上能得到什么。整个幼儿期父母对孩子肯定大过否定。上了小学，儿子的境地就不怎么从容了，上学的压力时时处处在影响着他，小家伙要承受各方面的压力，父母、老师、同学，太过我行我素、大而化之都是行不通的，比如没写作业的话，老师、家长的批评和提醒是少不了的，孩子在慢慢学着适应这种生活，烦恼也随之而来，这一阶段比较像格雷，虽然儿子的思维还没那么丰富，快乐和烦恼的花样都没那么多，但处境差不多，表扬和赞美不像以前那样轻易就能得到了。儿子青年时代会是什么样子我还不得而知，也不可想象，那种水到渠成的阶段要靠前面的积累，我希望自己到时候能平心静气，坦然接受，无论儿子成长成什么样子。

气味相投的好伙伴

★　上海市外国语大学附属第一实验中学，中预 10 班，沈昕仪 Elaine：《小屁孩日记》读来十分轻松。虽然没有用十分华丽的语言，却使我感受到了小屁孩那缤纷多彩的生活，给我带来无限的欢乐。那精彩的插图、幽默的文字实在是太有趣了，当中的故事在我们身边都有可能发生，让人身临其境。格雷总能说出我的心里话，他是和我有着共同语言的朋友。所以他们搞的恶作剧一直让我跃跃欲试，也想找一次机会尝试一下。不知别的读者怎么想，我觉得格雷挺喜欢出风头的。我也是这样的人，总怕别人无视了自己。当看到格雷蹦出那些稀奇古怪的点子的时候，我多想帮他一把啊——毕竟我们是"气味相投"的同类人嘛。另一方面，我身处在外语学校，时刻都需要积累英语单词，但这件事总是让我觉得枯燥乏味。而《小屁孩日记》帮了我的大忙：我在享受快乐阅读的同时，还可以对照中英文学到很多常用英语单词。我发现其实生活中还有很多事情值得我们去用笔写下来。即使是小事，这些童年的故事也是很值得我们回忆的。既然还生活在童年，还能够写下那些故事，又何乐而不为呢？

亲爱的读者，你看完这本书后，有什么感想吗？请来电话或是登录本书的博客与我们分享吧！等本书再版时，这里也许换上了你的读后感呢！

我们的电话号码是 020－83795744，博客地址是：blog. sina. com. cn/ wimpykid。

悦读 "小·屁孩"

《小·屁孩日记①——鬼屋创意》

在日记里，格雷记叙了他如何驾驭充满冒险的中学生活，如何巧妙逃脱学校歌唱比赛，最重要的是如何不让任何人发现他的秘密。他经常想捉弄人反被人捉弄；他常常想做好事却弄巧成拙；他屡屡身陷尴尬境遇竟逢"凶"化吉。他不是好孩子，也不是坏孩子，就只是普通的孩子；他有点自私，但重要关头也会挺身而出保护朋友……

《小·屁孩日记②——谁动了千年奶酪》

在《小屁孩日记②》里，主人公格雷度过一个没有任何奇迹发生的圣诞节。为打发漫长无聊的下雪天，他和死党罗利雄心勃勃地想要堆出"世界上最大的雪人"，却因为惹怒老爸，雪人被销毁；格雷可是不甘寂寞的，没几天，他又找到乐子了，在送幼儿园小朋友过街的时候，他制造了一起"虫子事件"吓唬小朋友，并嫁祸罗利，从而导致一场"严重"的友情危机……格雷能顺利化解危机，重新赢得好朋友罗利的信任吗？

《小·屁孩日记③——好孩子不撒谎》

在本册里，格雷开始了他的暑假生活。慢着，别以为他的假期会轻松愉快。其实他整个暑

假都被游泳训练班给毁了。他还自作聪明地导演了一出把同学齐拉格当成隐形人的闹剧，他以为神不知鬼不觉就可以每天偷吃姜饼，终于在圣诞前夜东窗事发，付出了巨大的代价……

《小·屁孩日记④——偷鸡不成蚀把米》

本集里，格雷仿佛落入了他哥哥罗德里克的魔掌中一般，怎么也逃脱不了厄运：他在老妈的威逼利诱下跟罗德里克学爵士鼓，却只能在一旁干看罗德里克自娱自乐；与好友罗利一起偷看罗德里克窝藏的鬼片，却不幸玩过火害罗利受伤，为此格雷不得不付出惨重代价——代替罗利在全校晚会上表演魔术——而他的全部表演内容就是为一个一年级小朋友递魔术道具。更大的悲剧还在后面，他不惜花"重金"购买罗德里克的旧作业想要蒙混过关，却不幸买到一份不及格的作业。最后，他暑假误入女厕所的囧事还被罗德里克在全校大肆宣扬……格雷还有脸在学校混吗？他的日记还能继续下去吗？

《小·屁孩日记⑤——午餐零食大盗》

格雷在新的一年里展开了他的学校生活：克雷格老师的词典不翼而飞，于是每天课间休息时所有同学都被禁止外出，直至字典被找到；格雷的午餐零食从糖果变成了两个水果，他怀疑是哥哥罗德里克偷了零食，誓要查出真相。因为午餐零食闹的"糖荒"，让格雷精神不振，总是在下午的课堂上打瞌睡。格雷没有多余的零用钱，不能自己买糖果，于是他想到了自己埋下的时光宝盒——里面放着三美元的钞票。格雷挖出时光宝盒，暂时缓解了"糖荒"。另一边厢，学校即将举行第一次的情人节舞会。格雷对漂亮的同班同学荷莉心仪已久，就决定趁舞会好好表现。在舞会上，他成功与荷莉互相交换了情人节卡片，并想邀请荷莉跳舞，于是他向人群中的荷莉走去……

《小·屁孩日记⑥——可怕的炮兵学校》

格雷想尽一切办法让老爸摆脱一些可怕的念头。格雷的老爸一直希望他能加强锻炼，就让他加入了周末的足球队。格雷在足球队吃尽了苦头：他先被教练派去当球童，在荆棘丛里捡球累了个半死；然后又被要求坐在寒风中观赛，冷得他直打哆嗦；后来他自以为聪明地选择了后备守门员的位置，最后却因为正选守门员受伤而不得不披挂上阵。在输掉足球比赛后，格雷觉得老爸因此而生气了。未想老爸又冒出另一个更可怕的念头：把格雷送进炮兵学校。格雷却自动请缨加入周末的童子军，因为这样一来他就不必再去参加足球训练了。然而，在童子军的父子营中，格雷又为老爸惹来麻烦……老爸决定在这个学期结束后，就立刻把格雷送进炮兵学校。眼看暑假就要开始了，格雷因此坐立不安……

《小·屁孩日记⑦——从天而降的巨债》

暑假刚开始，格雷就与老爸老妈展开了拉锯战：老爸老妈坚持认为孩子放暑假就应该到户外去活动，但格雷却宁愿躲在家里打游戏机、看肥皂剧。不得已之下，格雷跟着死党罗利到乡村俱乐部玩，两人在那儿吃了一点东西，就欠下了83美元的"巨债"。于是，他们不得不想尽一切办法打工还债……

他们能把债务还清吗？格雷又惹出了什么笑话？

《小·屁孩日记⑧——"头盖骨摇晃机"的幸存者》

老妈带全家上了旅行车，看到防晒霜和泳衣，格雷满心以为是去海滩度假，却原来只是去水上乐园——一个令格雷吃过很多苦头的地方，过去的不愉快记忆也就罢了，这次好不容易做好一切准备，广播却通知"因闪电天气停止营业"；回到家里又怎样呢？格雷发现他心爱的鱼惨遭罗德里克宠物鱼的"毒口"；盼望已久的小狗阿甜来了，非但不是补偿，反而使格雷的生活一团糟；格雷发现救生员是希尔斯小姐，这使得他一改对于小镇游泳场的糟糕看法，小心眼儿活动起来；妈妈安排了一个格雷与爸爸改善关系的机会，可是格雷却用"甲壳虫小姐"召来了警察，搞得老爸灰溜溜的，他们关系更僵；老妈处心积虑安排格雷和死党罗利的一家去了海滩，格雷却又惹了祸……

我们可爱又倒霉的格雷啊，他该如何处理这一切？"头盖骨摇晃机"又是怎么回事？